Curly scarf & Bubbles both in Big Wool

Spike in Big Wool

Frothy in Chunky Print

Embrace in Chunky Print & Biggy Print

Halle in Big Wool

Float in Big Wool

Swing in Big Wool

Tucker in Big Wool

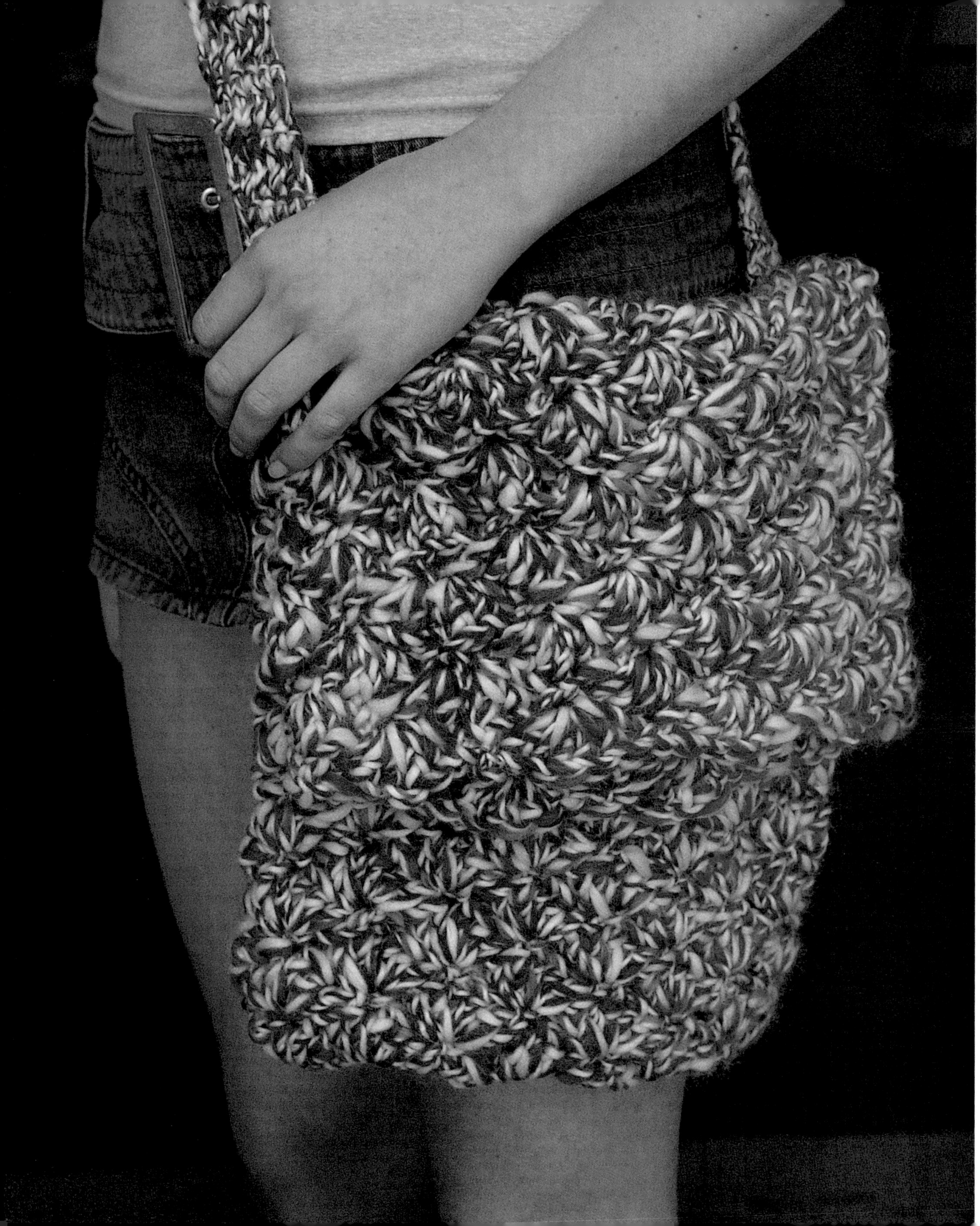

Poppy in Chunky Print

Violet in Big Wool

Berry & Spike hat both in Big Wool

Huddle in Chunky Print & Biggy Print

Crumble in Chunky Print

Bloom in Big Wool

Grit in Biggy Print & Molten in Chunky Print & Biggy Print

Major in Big Wool

Fran in Chunky Print

Iris in Big Wool & Foster in Chunky Print

Toast in Chunky Print

Trench in Big Wool, Steel in Biggy Print & Sweep in Chunky Print & Biggy Print

Twirl & Seth in Big Wool

Gaby in Big Wool

Halle in Big Wool & Murmur in Biggy Print

Lilly in Chunky Print & Huddle in Chunky Print & Biggy Print

Lily in Chunky Print

THE NEXT BIG THING

Index

BERRY

KIM HARGREAVES

YARN

	XS	S	M	L	XL	
To fit bust	81	86	91	97	102	cm
	32	34	36	38	40	in

Rowan Big Wool

	7	7	8	9	9	x 100gm

(photographed in Lucky 020)

NEEDLES

1 pair 10mm (no 000) (US 15) needles
1 pair 12mm (US 17) needles

BUTTONS

6 x 75336

TENSION

8 sts and 12 rows to 10 cm measured over stocking stitch, 9 sts and 10 rows to 10 cm measured over trinity stitch using 12mm (US 17) needles.

BACK

Cast on 33 (35: 37: 39: 41) sts using 10mm (US 15) needles.
Row 1 (RS): K0 (0: 0: 0: 1), P0 (1: 2: 3: 3), *K3, P3, rep from * to last 3 (4: 5: 0: 1) sts, K3 (3: 3: 0: 1), P0 (1: 2: 0: 0).

Row 2: P0 (0: 0: 0: 1), K0 (1: 2: 3: 3), *P3, K3, rep from * to last 3 (4: 5: 0: 1) sts, P3 (3: 3: 0: 1), K0 (1: 2: 0: 0).
These 2 rows form rib.
Work in rib for a further 8 rows, ending with a WS row.
Change to 12mm (US 17) needles.
Beg with a K row, cont in st st, shaping side seams by inc 1 st at each end of 3rd and foll 10th row. 37 (39: 41: 43: 45) sts.
Cont straight until back measures 32 (33: 33: 34: 34) cm, ending with a WS row.
Shape armholes
Cast off 3 sts at beg of next 2 rows.
31 (33: 35: 37: 39) sts.
Dec 1 st at each end of next 2 (2: 3: 3: 4) rows.
27 (29: 29: 31: 31) sts.
Cont straight until armhole measures 20 (20: 21: 21: 22) cm, ending with a WS row.
Shape shoulders and back neck
Cast off 3 sts at beg of next 2 rows.
21 (23: 23: 25: 25) sts.
Next row (RS): Cast off 3 sts, K until there are 5 (6: 6: 6: 6) sts on right needle and turn, leaving rem sts on a holder.
Work each side of neck separately.
Cast off 3 sts at beg of next row.
Cast off rem 2 (3: 3: 3: 3) sts.
With RS facing, rejoin yarn to rem sts, cast off centre 5 (5: 5: 7: 7) sts, K to end.
Complete to match first side, reversing shapings.

LEFT FRONT

Cast on 17 (18: 19: 20: 21) sts using 10mm (US 15) needles.
Row 1 (RS): K0 (0: 0: 0: 1), P0 (1: 2: 3: 3), *K3, P3, rep from * to last 5 sts, K3, P2.
Row 2: K2, *P3, K3, rep from * to last 3 (4: 5: 0: 1) sts, P3 (3: 3: 0: 1), K0 (1: 2: 0: 0).
These 2 rows form rib.
Work in rib for a further 7 rows, ending with a RS row.
Row 10 (WS): (Rib 6, M1) twice, rib to end.
19 (20: 21: 22: 23) sts.
Change to 12mm (US 17) needles.
Cont in trinity st as folls:
Row 1 (RS): Purl.
Row 2: *(K1, P1, K1) all into next st, P3tog, rep from * to last 3 (0: 1: 2: 3) sts, K3 (0: 1: 2: 3).
Row 3: Inc in first st, P to end.
20 (21: 22: 23: 24) sts.

Row 4: *P3tog, (K1, P1, K1) all into next st, rep from * to last 0 (1: 2: 3: 0) sts, K0 (1: 2: 3: 0).
These 4 rows form trinity st and start side seam shaping.
Cont in trinity st, shaping side seam by inc 1 st at beg of 7th row. 21 (22: 23: 24: 25) sts.
Cont straight until left front **measures** same as back to beg of armhole shaping, ending with a WS row.
Shape armhole
Keeping patt correct, cast off 3 sts at beg of next row. 18 (19: 20: 21: 22) sts.
Work 1 row.
Dec 1 st at armhole edge of next 3 (3: 4: 4: 5) rows.
15 (16: 16: 17: 17) sts.
Cont straight until armhole measures 13 (13: 14: 14: 15) cm, ending with a **RS** row.
Shape neck
Keeping patt correct, cast off 3 (3: 3: 4: 4) sts at beg of next row. 12 (13: 13: 13: 13) sts.
Dec 1 st at neck edge of next 3 rows, then on foll alt row. 8 (9: 9: 9: 9) sts.
Work a few rows straight until left front **measures** same as back to start of shoulder shaping, ending with a WS row.
Shape shoulder
Cast off 3 sts at beg of next and foll alt row.
Work 1 row.
Cast off rem 2 (3: 3: 3: 3) sts.

RIGHT FRONT

Cast on 17 (18: 19: 20: 21) sts using 10mm (US 15) needles.
Row 1 (RS): P2, *K3, P3, rep from * to last 3 (4: 5: 0: 1) sts, K3 (3: 3: 0: 1), P0 (1: 2: 0: 0).
Row 2: P0 (0: 0: 0: 1), K0 (1: 2: 3: 3), *P3, K3, rep from * to last 5 sts, P3, K2.
These 2 rows form rib.
Work in rib for a further 7 rows, ending with a RS row.
Row 10 (WS): Rib to last 12 sts, (M1, rib 6) twice. 19 (20: 21: 22: 23) sts.
Change to 12mm (US 17) needles.
Cont in trinity st as folls:
Row 1 (RS): Purl.
Row 2: K3 (0: 1: 2: 3), *P3tog, (K1, P1, K1) all into next st, rep from * to end.
Row 3: P to last st, inc in last st.
20 (21: 22: 23: 24) sts.
Row 4: K0 (1: 2: 3: 0), *(K1, P1, K1) all into next st, P3tog, rep from * to end.

These 4 rows form trinity st and start side seam shaping.

Complete to match left front, reversing shapings.

SLEEVES (both alike)

Cast on 23 (23: 23: 25: 25) sts using 10mm (US 15) needles.

Row 1 (RS): P1 (1: 1: 2: 2), ★K3, P3, rep from ★ to last 4 (4: 4: 5: 5) sts, K3, P1 (1: 1: 2: 2).

Row 2: K1 (1: 1: 2: 2), ★P3, K3, rep from ★ to last 4 (4: 4: 5: 5) sts, P3, K1 (1: 1: 2: 2).

These 2 rows form rib.

Work in rib for a further 8 rows, ending with a WS row.

Change to 12mm (US 17) needles.

Beg with a K row, cont in st st, shaping sides by inc 1 st at each end of 7th and foll 16th row. 27 (27: 27: 29: 29) sts.

Cont straight until sleeve measures 43 (43: 44: 44: 44) cm, ending with a WS row.

Shape top

Cast off 3 sts at beg of next 2 rows. 21 (21: 21: 23: 23) sts.

Dec 1 st at each end of next and foll alt row, then on every foll 4th row until 13 (13: 13: 15: 15) sts rem.

Work 1 row.

Dec 1 st at each end of next and foll 0 (0: 0: 1: 1) alt row, then on foll row, ending with a WS row.

Cast off rem 9 sts.

MAKING UP

PRESS as described on the information page. Join both shoulder seams using back stitch, or mattress st if preferred.

Button band

With RS facing and using 10mm (US 15) needles, pick up and knit 41 sts down left front opening edge, between neck shaping and cast-on edge.

Row 1 (WS): K1, ★P3, K3, rep from ★ to last 4 sts, P3, K1.

Row 2: K4, ★P3, K3, rep from ★ to last st, K1.

These 2 rows form rib.

Work in rib for a further 3 rows. Cast off in rib.

Buttonhole band

Work as given for button band, picking up sts up right front opening edge and with the addition of 6 buttonholes worked in row 3 as folls:

Row 3 (buttonhole row) (WS): Rib 1, ★work 2 tog, yrn (to make a buttonhole), rib 5, rep from ★ to last 5 sts, work 2 tog, yrn (to make 6th buttonhole) rib 3.

Collar

With RS facing and using 10mm (US 15) needles, starting and ending halfway across top of bands, pick up and knit 12 (12: 12: 14: 14) sts up right side of neck, 11 (11: 11: 13: 13) sts from back, and 12 (12: 12: 14: 14) sts down left side of neck. 35 (35: 35: 41: 41) sts.

Beg with row 2, work in rib as given for button band for 11 cm.

Cast off in rib.

See information page for finishing instructions, setting in sleeves using the set-in method.

EMBRACE

KIM HARGREAVES

YARN

	XS	S	M	L	XL	
To fit bust	81	86	91	97	102	cm
	32	34	36	38	40	in

Rowan Chunky Print and Biggy Print

A Chunky Print	Woolly	071				
	10	10	11	11	12	x 100gm
B Biggy Print	Swirl	250				
	2	2	2	3	3	x 100gm

NEEDLES

1 pair 7mm (no 2) (US 10½) needles
1 pair 8mm (no 0) (US 11) needles

TENSION

11 sts and 14 rows to 10 cm measured over reverse stocking stitch using 8mm (US 11) needles.

SPECIAL ABBREVIATIONS

Loop 1 = Using yarn B, K next st leaving st on left needle, bring yarn forward between needles and wrap it twice round thumb of left hand, take yarn between needles to back of work and K same st again, slipping st off left needle. Bring yarn forward between needles and back over needle to WS of work. Lift the 2 sts just made over this loop

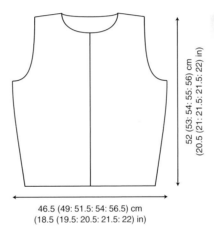

52 (53: 54: 55: 56) cm
(20.5 (21: 21.5: 21.5: 22) in)

46.5 (49: 51.5: 54: 56.5) cm
(18.5 (19.5: 20.5: 21.5: 22) in)

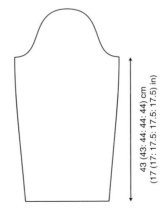

43 (43: 44: 44: 44) cm
(17 (17: 17.5: 17.5: 17.5) in)

BACK

Cast on 57 (59: 63: 65: 69) sts using 7mm (US 10½) needles and yarn A.

Beg with a P row, work in rev st st for 6 rows, ending with a WS row.

Change to 8mm (US 11) needles.

Cont in rev st st until back measures 46 cm, ending with a WS row.

Shape raglan armholes

Cast off 5 sts at beg of next 2 rows.

47 (49: 53: 55: 59) sts.

Extra small size only

Next row (RS): P2, P2tog, P to last 4 sts, P2tog tbl, P2. 45 sts.

Work 3 rows.

Medium, large and extra large sizes only

Next row (RS): P2, P2tog, P to last 4 sts, P2tog tbl, P2.

Next row: K2, K2tog tbl, K to last 4 sts, K2tog, K2.

Rep last 2 rows – (–: 0: 0: 1) times more.

– (–: 49: 51: 51) sts.

All sizes

Next row (RS): P2, P2tog, P to last 4 sts, P2tog tbl, P2.

Next row: Knit.

Rep last 2 rows 11 (13: 13: 13: 13) times more.

21 (21: 21: 23: 23) sts.

Next row (RS): P2, P2tog, P to last 4 sts, P2tog tbl, P2.

Next row: K2, K2tog tbl, K to last 4 sts, K2tog, K2.

Cast off rem 17 (17: 17: 19: 19) sts.

FRONT

Work as given for back until 29 (29: 29: 31: 31) sts rem in raglan shaping.

Work 1 row, ending with a WS row.

Shape front neck

Next row (RS): P2, P2tog, P3 and turn, leaving rem sts on a holder.

Work each side of neck separately.

Next row: K2tog, K4.

Next row: P2, P3tog.

Next row: K3.

Next row: P3tog.

Next row: K1 and fasten off.

With RS facing, rejoin yarn to rem sts, cast off centre 15 (15: 15: 17: 17) sts, P to last 4 sts, P2tog tbl, P2.

Next row: K4, K2tog.

Next row: P3tog tbl, P2.

Next row: K3.

Next row: P3tog tbl.

Next row: K1 and fasten off.

SLEEVES

Cast on 37 (39: 39: 41: 41) sts using 8mm (US 11) needles and yarn A.

Knit 1 row.

Cont in loop st patt as folls:

Join in yarn B.

Row 1 (RS): Using yarn A K1, *using yarn B loop 1, using yarn A K1, rep from * to end.

Row 2: Using yarn A knit.

Row 3: Using yarn A K2, *using yarn B loop 1, using yarn A K1, rep from * to last st, using yarn A K1.

Row 4: Using yarn A knit.

These 4 rows form loop st patt.

Work in loop st patt for a further 10 rows, ending with a WS row.

Beg with a P row, cont in rev st st using yarn A only as folls:

Inc 1 st at each end of 3rd and every foll 8th (10th: 8th: 10th: 8th) row to 45 (43: 49: 47: 51) sts, then on every foll 6th (8th: 6th: 8th: 6th) row until there are 51 (51: 53: 53: 55) sts.

Cont straight until sleeve measures 47 (47: 48: 48: 48) cm, ending with a WS row.

Shape raglan

Cast off 5 sts at beg of next 2 rows.

41 (41: 43: 43: 45) sts.

Working all raglan decreases as set by back, dec 1 st at each end of next and every foll alt row until 15 sts rem.

Work 1 row, ending with a WS row.

Left sleeve only

Dec 1 st at each end of next row.

13 sts.

Cast off 3 sts at beg of next row.

10 sts.

Dec 1 st at beg of next row. 9 sts.

Cast off 4 sts at beg and dec 1 st at end of next row.

Right sleeve only

Cast off 4 sts at beg and dec 1 st at end of next row.

Work 1 row.

Rep last 2 rows once more.

Both sleeves

Cast off rem 4 sts.

MAKING UP

PRESS as described on the information page.

Join raglan seams using back stitch, or mattress st if preferred.

Collar

Cast on 69 (69: 69: 73: 73) sts using 8mm (US 11) needles and yarn A.

Knit 1 row.

Join in yarn B and work in loop st patt for 4 rows, ending with a WS row.

Beg with a P row, cont in rev st st using yarn A only until collar measures 20 cm.

Cast off.

Join back seam of collar. Positioning collar seam at centre back neck, sew cast-off edge of collar to neck edge.

See information page for finishing instructions. If desired, carefully cut through loops of yarn B to form shaggy fringe effect.

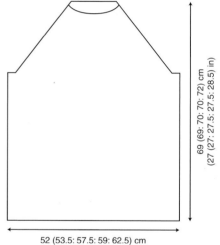

69 (69: 70: 70: 72) cm
(27 (27: 27.5: 27.5: 28.5) in)

52 (53.5: 57.5: 59: 62.5) cm
(20.5 (21: 22.5: 23: 24.5) in)

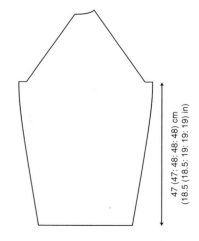

47 (47: 48: 48: 48) cm
(18.5 (18.5: 19: 19: 19) in)

TWIRL

KIM HARGREAVES

YARN

Self-fringed version
Rowan Big Wool
Bohemian   028   9   x   100gm
Contrast-fringed version
Rowan Big Wool
Sugar Spun   016   7   x   100gm
Rowan Biggy Print
Sheep   258   3   x   100gm

NEEDLES

1 pair 10mm (no 000) (US 15) needles
1 pair 12mm (US 17) needles

TENSION

8 sts and 12 rows to 10 cm measured over stocking stitch using 12mm (US 17) needles.

SPECIAL ABBREVIATION

Dec 2 = Slip next 2 sts as though to K2tog (marked st is 2nd of these sts), K1, pass 2 slipped sts over - 2 sts decreased.

Pattern note: As row end edges form actual finished front opening edges of garment, it is important these edges are kept neat. Therefore avoid joining in new balls of yarn at these edges.

BACK

Cast on 117 sts using 12mm (US 17) needles. Place marker on centre st.
Row 1 (RS): (P1, K1) 28 times, P1, dec 2, P1, (K1, P1) to end.
Row 2: (P1, K1) to marked st, P marked st, (K1, P1) to end.
These 2 rows form moss st.
Row 3: Moss st to within 1 st of marked st, dec 2, moss st to end.
Row 4: Moss st to marked st, P marked st, moss st to end.
Rows 5 and 6: As rows 3 and 4. 111 sts.
Row 7 (RS): K to within 1 st of marked st, dec 2, K to end. 109 sts.
Row 8: Purl.
Rows 7 and 8 set the sts - st st with 2 sts decreased at centre of every RS row.
Dec 1 st at each end of 11th and foll 12th row, then on foll 10th row, then on foll 8th row, then on foll 6th row, then on 2 foll 4th rows, then on 3 foll alt rows, then on foll row **and at same time** dec 2 sts as set at centre of every RS row, ending with a WS row. 25 sts.
Next row (RS): Cast off 3 sts, K to within 1 st of marked st, dec 2, K to end.
Next row: Cast off 3 sts, P to end.
Cast off rem 17 sts.

FRONT

Work as given for back until 65 sts rem.
Work 1 row, ending with a WS row.
Divide for front opening
Next row (RS): K30, K2tog tbl and turn, leaving rem sts on a holder. 31 sts.
Work each side of neck separately.
Work 1 row.
Next row (RS): K2tog, K to last 2 sts, K2tog tbl. 29 sts.
Working all decreases as set by last row, dec 1 st at front opening edge of 2nd and foll 5 alt rows **and at same time** dec 1 st at side edge of 4th and foll 4th row, ending with a RS row. 21 sts.
Shape neck
Cast off 5 sts at beg of next row, dec 1 st at beg of foll row, then cast off 4 sts at beg of next row. 11 sts.

Dec 1 st at neck edge of next 4 rows **and at same time** dec 1 st at side edge of next and foll alt row, ending with a WS row. 5 sts.
Dec 1 st at side edge of next 2 rows.
Cast off rem 3 sts.
With RS facing, rejoin yarn to rem sts, K3tog, K to end. 31 sts.
Work 1 row.
Next row (RS): K2tog, K to last 2 sts, K2tog. 29 sts.
Working all decreases as set by last row, complete to match first side, reversing shapings.

MAKING UP

PRESS as described on the information page. Join both shoulder and side seams using back stitch, or mattress st if preferred.
Neck edging
With RS facing and using 10mm (US 15) needles, pick up and knit 15 sts up right side of neck, 17 sts from back, and 15 sts down left side of neck. 47 sts.
Cast off knitwise (on WS).
See information page for finishing instructions.
Make two 55 cm long twisted cords and attach one to each end of neck edging to form ties.
Cut 25 cm lengths of yarn and knot pairs of these lengths through cast-on edge to form fringe, placing knots on every other st.

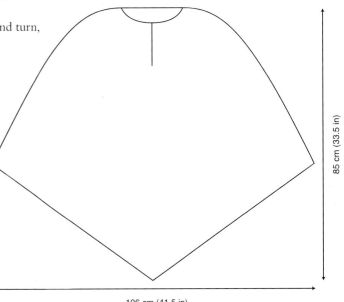

85 cm (33.5 in)

106 cm (41.5 in)

TRENCH

KIM HARGREAVES

YARN

	XS	S	M	L	XL	
To fit bust	81	86	91	97	102	cm
	32	34	36	38	40	in

Rowan Big Wool

	11	12	13	13	14	x 100gm

(photographed in Latte 018)

NEEDLES

1 pair 10mm (no 000) (US 15) needles
1 pair 12mm (US 17) needles

BUTTONS - 11 x 75334

TENSION

8 sts and 12 rows to 10 cm measured over
stocking stitch using 12mm (US 17) needles.

BACK

Cast on 43 (45: 47: 49: 51) sts using 10mm
(US 15) needles.
Row 1 (RS): P2 (0: 0: 0: 0), K3 (0: 1: 2: 3), *P3,
K3, rep from * to last 2 (3: 4: 5: 0) sts, P2 (3: 3:
3: 0), K0 (0: 1: 2: 0).
Row 2: K2 (0: 0: 0: 0), P3 (0: 1: 2: 3), *K3, P3,
rep from * to last 2 (3: 4: 5: 0) sts, K2 (3: 3: 3: 0),
P0 (0: 1: 2: 0).

These 2 rows form rib.
Work in rib for a further 8 rows, inc 1 st at end
of last row and ending with a WS row.
44 (46: 48: 50: 52) sts.
Change to 12mm (US 17) needles.
Cont in patt as folls:
Row 1 (RS): Knit.
Row 2: P2 (1: 2: 1: 2), *yrn, P2, then lift the yrn
over the last 2 sts and off right needle, P2, rep
from * to last 2 (1: 2: 1: 2) sts, P2 (1: 2: 1: 2).
Row 3: Knit.
Row 4: P2 (1: 2: 1: 2), *P2, yrn, P2, then lift the
yrn over the last 2 sts and off right needle, rep
from * to last 2 (1: 2: 1: 2) sts, P2 (1: 2: 1: 2).
These 4 rows form patt.
Cont in patt until back measures 74 (75: 75: 76:
76) cm, ending with a WS row.
Shape armholes
Keeping patt correct, cast off 3 sts at beg of next
2 rows. 38 (40: 42: 44: 46) sts.
Dec 1 st at each end of next 4 (4: 5: 5: 6) rows.
30 (32: 32: 34: 34) sts.
Cont straight until armhole measures 25 (25: 26:
26: 27) cm, ending with a WS row.
Shape shoulders and back neck
Cast off 3 sts at beg of next 2 rows.
24 (26: 26: 28: 28) sts.
Next row (RS): Cast off 3 sts, K until there are
5 (6: 6: 6: 6) sts on right needle and turn, leaving
rem sts on a holder.
Work each side of neck separately.
Cast off 3 sts at beg of next row.
Cast off rem 2 (3: 3: 3: 3) sts.
With RS facing, rejoin yarn to rem sts, cast off
centre 8 (8: 8: 10: 10) sts, K to end.
Complete to match first side, reversing shapings.

POCKET LININGS (make 2)
Cast on 12 sts using 12mm (US 17) needles.
Beg with a K row, work in st st for 18 rows,
ending with a WS row.
Break yarn and leave sts on a holder.

LEFT FRONT
Cast on 21 (22: 23: 24: 25) sts using 10mm
(US 15) needles.
Row 1 (RS): P2 (0: 0: 0: 0), K3 (0: 1: 2: 3), *P3,
K3, rep from * to last 4 sts, P3, K1.
Row 2: P1, *K3, P3, rep from * to last 2 (3: 4:
5: 0) sts, K2 (3: 3: 3: 0), P0 (0: 1: 2: 0).
These 2 rows form rib.

Work in rib for a further 8 rows, ending with a
WS row.
Change to 12mm (US 17) needles.
Cont in patt as folls:
Row 1 (RS): Knit.
Row 2: P3 (1: 1: 3: 3), *yrn, P2, then lift the yrn
over the last 2 sts and off right needle, P2, rep
from * to last 2 (1: 2: 1: 2) sts, P2 (1: 2: 1: 2).
Row 3: Knit.
Row 4: P1, (yrn, P2, then lift the yrn over the
last 2 sts and off right needle) 1 (0: 0: 1: 1) times,
*P2, yrn, P2, then lift the yrn over the last 2 sts
and off right needle, rep from * to last 2 (1: 2:
1: 2) sts, P2 (1: 2: 1: 2).
These 4 rows form patt.
Cont in patt until left front measures 42 (43: 43:
44: 44) cm, ending with a WS row.
Place pocket
Next row (RS): K4 (5: 6: 7: 8), slip next 12 sts
onto a holder and, in their place, K across 12 sts
of first pocket lining, K to end.
Cont straight until left front matches back to
beg of armhole shaping, ending with a WS row.
Shape armhole
Keeping patt correct, cast off 3 sts at beg of next
row. 18 (19: 20: 21: 22) sts.
Work 1 row.
Dec 1 st at armhole edge of next 4 (4: 5: 5: 6) rows.
14 (15: 15: 16: 16) sts.
Cont straight until 6 rows less have been worked
than on back to start of shoulder shaping, ending
with a WS row.
Shape neck
Next row (RS): K11 (12: 12: 12: 12) and turn,
leaving rem 3 (3: 3: 4: 4) sts on a holder.
Dec 1 st at neck edge of next 2 rows, then on
foll alt row. 8 (9: 9: 9: 9) sts.
Work 1 row, ending with a WS row.
Shape shoulder
Cast off 3 sts at beg of next and foll alt row.
Work 1 row.
Cast off rem 2 (3: 3: 3: 3) sts.

RIGHT FRONT
Cast on 21 (22: 23: 24: 25) sts using 10mm
(US 15) needles.
Row 1 (RS): K1, *P3, K3, rep from * to last
2 (3: 4: 5: 0) sts, P2 (3: 3: 3: 0), K0 (0: 1: 2: 0).
Row 2: K2 (0: 0: 0: 0), P3 (0: 1: 2: 3), *K3, P3,
rep from * to last 4 sts, K3, P1.
These 2 rows form rib.

Work in rib for 8 rows, ending with a WS row.
Change to 12mm (US 17) needles.
Cont in patt as folls:
Row 1 (RS): Knit.
Row 2: P3 (1: 1: 3: 3), ★yrn, P2, then lift the yrn over the last 2 sts and off right needle, P2, rep from ★ to last 2 (1: 2: 1: 2) sts, P2 (1: 2: 1: 2).
Row 3: Knit.
Row 4: P1, (yrn, P2, then lift the yrn over the last 2 sts and off right needle) 1 (0: 0: 1: 1) times, ★P2, yrn, P2, then lift the yrn over the last 2 sts and off right needle, rep from ★ to last 2 (1: 2: 1: 2) sts, P2 (1: 2: 1: 2).
These 4 rows form patt.
Complete to match left front, reversing shapings and placing pocket as folls:
Place pocket
Next row (RS): K5, slip next 12 sts onto a holder and, in their place, K across 12 sts of second pocket lining, K to end.

SLEEVES (both alike)
Cast on 25 (25: 27: 27: 27) sts using 10mm (US 15) needles.
Row 1 (RS): P2 (2: 2: 3: 3), ★K3, P3, rep from ★ to last 5 (5: 5: 6: 6) sts, K3, P2 (2: 2: 3: 3).
Row 2: K2 (2: 2: 3: 3), ★P3, K3, rep from ★ to last 5 (5: 5: 6: 6) sts, P3, K2 (2: 2: 3: 3).
These 2 rows form rib.
Work in rib for a further 8 rows, inc 1 st at end of last row and ending with a WS row.
26 (26: 28: 28: 28) sts.
Change to 12mm (US 17) needles.
Cont in patt as folls:
Row 1 (RS): Knit.
Row 2: P1 (1: 2: 2: 2), ★yrn, P2, then lift the yrn over the last 2 sts and off right needle, P2, rep from ★ to last 1 (1: 2: 2: 2) sts, P1 (1: 2: 2: 2).
Row 3: Knit.
Row 4: P1 (1: 2: 2: 2), ★P2, yrn, P2, then lift the yrn over the last 2 sts and off right needle, rep from ★ to last 1 (1: 2: 2: 2) sts, P1 (1: 2: 2: 2).
These 4 rows form patt.
Cont in patt, shaping sides by inc 1 st at each end of 5th and foll 18th row. 30 (30: 32: 32: 32) sts.
Cont straight until sleeve measures 45 (45: 46: 46: 46) cm, ending with a WS row.
Shape top
Keeping patt correct, cast off 3 sts at beg of next 2 rows. 24 (24: 26: 26: 26) sts.
Dec 1 st at each end of next and foll alt row,

then on every foll 4th row until 14 (14: 16: 16: 16) sts rem.
Work 1 row.
Dec 1 st at each end of next and foll 0 (0: 1: 1: 1) alt row, then on foll row, ending with a WS row.
Cast off rem 10 sts.

MAKING UP
PRESS as described on the information page.
Join both shoulder seams using back stitch.
Button band
Cast on 5 sts using 10mm (US 15) needles.
Row 1 (RS): K1, (P1, K1) twice.
Row 2: As row 1.
These 2 rows form moss st.
Cont in moss st until band, when slightly stretched, fits up left front opening edge, from cast-on edge to neck shaping, ending with a WS row.
Break yarn and leave sts on a holder.
Slip stitch band in place. Mark positions for 7 buttons on this band - first to come 30 cm up from cast-on edge, last to come 2 cm below neck shaping and rem 5 buttons evenly spaced between.
Buttonhole band
Work as given for button band, with the addition of 7 buttonholes worked to correspond with positions marked for buttons as folls:
Buttonhole row (RS): K1, P1, yrn, P2tog, K1.
Slip stitch band in place.
Collar
With RS facing and using 10mm (US 15) needles, slip 5 sts of buttonhole band and then 3 (3: 3: 4: 4) sts from right front holder onto right needle, rejoin yarn and pick up and knit 11 (11: 11: 12: 12) sts up right side of neck, 17 (17: 17: 19: 19) sts from back, and 11 (11: 11: 12: 12) sts down left side of neck, then K 3 (3: 3: 4: 4) sts from left front holder, and moss st 5 sts from button band. 55 (55: 55: 61: 61) sts.
Row 1 (RS of collar, WS of body): Moss st 5 sts, K3, ★P3, K3, rep from ★ to last 5 sts, moss st 5 sts.
Row 2: Moss st 5 sts, P3, ★K3, P3, rep from ★ to last 5 sts, moss st 5 sts.
Rep these 2 rows until collar measures 25 cm.
Cast off in patt.
Pocket tops (both alike)
Slip 12 sts from pocket holder onto 10mm (US 15) needles and rejoin yarn with RS facing.
Knit 2 rows.
Cast off knitwise (on WS).

Pocket flaps (make 2)
Cast on 15 sts using 10mm (US 15) needles.
Row 1 (RS): P3, (K3, P3) twice.
Row 2: K3, (P3, K3) twice.
These 2 rows form rib.
Work in rib for a further 2 rows, ending with a WS row.
Row 5 (RS): P3, K2tog, yfwd, K1, P3, K1, yfwd, K2tog tbl, P3.
Cont in rib until pocket flap measures 11 cm.
Cast off in rib.
Position pocket flap above pocket opening using photograph as a guide and stitch cast-off edge in place. Attach buttons to pockets to correspond with buttonholes in flaps.
See information page for finishing instructions, setting in sleeves using the set-in method.

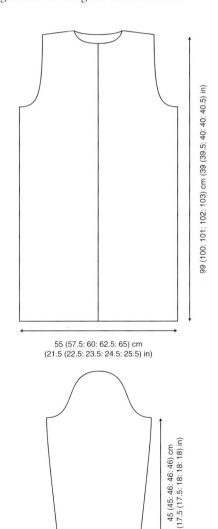

99 (100: 101: 102: 103) cm (39 (39.5: 40: 40: 40.5) in)

55 (57.5: 60: 62.5: 65) cm (21.5 (22.5: 23.5: 24.5: 25.5) in)

45 (45: 46: 46: 46) cm (17.5 (17.5: 18: 18: 18) in)

SETH

KIM HARGREAVES

YARN

	S	M	L	XL	XXL
To fit chest	97	102	107	112	117 cm
	38	40	42	44	46 in

Rowan Big Wool

| | 10 | 10 | 11 | 12 | 12 | x 100gm |

(photographed in Blue Velvet 026)

NEEDLES

1 pair 10mm (no 000) (US 15) needles
1 pair 12mm (US 17) needles
Cable needle

TENSION

8 sts and 12 rows to 10 cm measured over reverse stocking stitch using 12mm (US 17) needles.

SPECIAL ABBREVIATIONS

C6B = Cable 6 back Slip next 3 sts onto cable needle and leave at back of work, K3, then K3 from cable needle

C6F = Cable 6 front Slip next 3 sts onto cable needle and leave at front of work, K3, then K3 from cable needle

Cr4R = Cross 4 right Slip next st onto cable needle and leave at back of work, K3, then P1 from cable needle

Cr4L = Cross 4 left Slip next 3 sts onto cable needle and leave at front of work, P1, then K3 from cable needle

BACK

Cast on 55 (57: 59: 61: 63) sts using 10mm (US 15) needles.
Row 1 (RS): P0 (0: 0: 0: 1), K0 (1: 2: 3: 3), (P3, K3) twice, P2, (K3, P3) 4 times, K3, P2, (K3, P3) twice, K0 (1: 2: 3: 3), P0 (0: 0: 0: 1).
Row 2: K0 (0: 0: 0: 1), P0 (1: 2: 3: 3), (K3, P3) twice, K2, (P3, K3) 4 times, P3, K2, (P3, K3) twice, P0 (1: 2: 3: 3), K0 (0: 0: 0: 1).
These 2 rows form rib.
Work in rib for a further 6 rows, ending with a WS row.
Change to 12mm (US 17) needles.
Cont in cable patt as folls:
Row 1 (RS): P9 (10: 11: 12: 13), Cr4L, Cr4R, P21, Cr4L, Cr4R, P to end.
Row 2: K10 (11: 12: 13: 14), P6, K23, P6, K to end.
Row 3: P10 (11: 12: 13: 14), C6B, P23, C6F, P to end.
Row 4: As row 2.
Row 5: P9 (10: 11: 12: 13), Cr4R, Cr4L, P21, Cr4R, Cr4L, P to end.
Row 6: K9 (10: 11: 12: 13), P3, K2, P3, K21, P3, K2, P3, K to end.
Row 7: P9 (10: 11: 12: 13), K3, P2, K3, P21, K3, P2, K3, P to end.
Rows 8 to 11: As rows 6 and 7, twice.
Row 12: As row 6.
These 12 rows form patt.
Cont in patt until back measures 38 (38: 39: 39: 40) cm, ending with a WS row.

Shape armholes
Keeping patt correct, cast off 4 sts at beg of next 2 rows.
47 (49: 51: 53: 55) sts.
Cont straight until armhole measures 27 (28: 28: 29: 29) cm, ending with a WS row.

Shape shoulders and back neck
Cast off 5 (5: 6: 6: 6) sts at beg of next 2 rows.
37 (39: 39: 41: 43) sts.
Next row (RS): Cast off 5 (5: 6: 6: 6) sts, patt until there are 8 (9: 8: 8: 9) sts on right needle and turn, leaving rem sts on a holder.
Work each side of neck separately.
Cast off 3 sts at beg of next row.
Cast off rem 5 (6: 5: 5: 6) sts.

With RS facing, rejoin yarn to rem sts, cast off centre 11 (11: 11: 13: 13) sts, patt to end.
Complete to match first side, reversing shapings.

FRONT

Work as given for back until 6 rows less have been worked than on back to start of shoulder shaping, ending with a WS row.
Shape front neck
Next row (RS): Patt 19 (20: 21: 21: 22) sts and turn, leaving rem sts on a holder.
Work each side of neck separately.
Dec 1 st at neck edge of next 3 rows, then on foll alt row, ending with a WS row.
15 (16: 17: 17: 18) sts.
Shape shoulder
Cast off 5 (5: 6: 6: 6) sts at beg of next and foll alt row.
Work 1 row.
Cast off rem 5 (6: 5: 5: 6) sts.
With RS facing, rejoin yarn to rem sts, cast off centre 9 (9: 9: 11: 11) sts, patt to end.
Complete to match first side, reversing shapings.

SLEEVES (both alike)

Cast on 29 (29: 31: 31: 31) sts using 10mm (US 15) needles.
Row 1 (RS): K1 (1: 2: 2: 2), *P3, K3, rep from * to last 4 (4: 5: 5: 5) sts, P3, K1 (1: 2: 2: 2).
Row 2: P1 (1: 2: 2: 2), *K3, P3, rep from * to last 4 (4: 5: 5: 5) sts, K3, P1 (1: 2: 2: 2).
These 2 rows form rib.
Work in rib for a further 6 rows, ending with a WS row.
Change to 12mm (US 17) needles.
Beg with a P row, cont in rev st st, shaping sides by inc 1 st at each end of 7th (5th: 7th: 7th: 7th) and every foll 6th row to 41 (45: 41: 47: 47) sts, then on every foll 8th (-: 8th: -: -) row until there are 43 (-: 45: -: -) sts.
Cont straight until sleeve measures 54 (55: 55: 56: 56) cm, ending with a WS row.
Cast off.

MAKING UP

PRESS as described on the information page.
Join right shoulder seam using back stitch, or mattress st if preferred.
Neckband
With RS facing and using 10mm (US 15) needles, pick up and knit 8 (8: 8: 9: 9) sts down

left side of neck, 9 (9: 9: 11: 11) sts from front,
8 (8: 8: 9: 9) sts up right side of neck, then
17 (17: 17: 19: 19) sts from back.
42 (42: 42: 48: 48) sts.
Row 1 (WS): ★K3, P3, rep from ★ to end.
Rep this row until neckband measures 6 cm.
Cast off in rib.
See information page for finishing instructions,
setting in sleeves using the square set-in method.

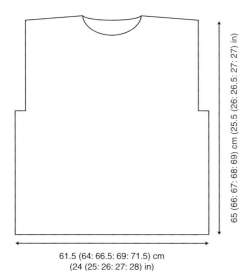

65 (66: 67: 68: 69) cm (25.5 (26: 26.5: 27: 27) in)

61.5 (64: 66.5: 69: 71.5) cm
(24 (25: 26: 27: 28) in)

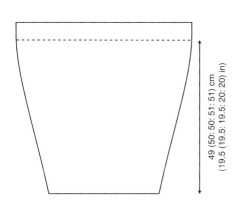

49 (50: 50: 51: 51) cm
(19.5 (19.5: 19.5: 20: 20) in)

TUCKER

KIM HARGREAVES

YARN

	XS	S	M	L	XL
To fit bust	81	86	91	97	102 cm
	32	34	36	38	40 in

Rowan Big Wool

| | 11 | 11 | 12 | 13 | 13 x 100gm |

(photographed in Best Brown 027)

NEEDLES

1 pair 10mm (no 000) (US 15) needles
1 pair 12mm (US 17) needles

TENSION

8 sts and 12 rows to 10 cm measured over
stocking stitch, 9 sts and 10 rows to 10 cm
measured over trinity stitch using 12mm (US 17)
needles.

BACK

Cast on 48 (52: 52: 56: 60) sts using 12mm
(US 17) needles.
Row 1 (RS): Purl.
Row 2: ★(K1, P1, K1) all into next st, P3tog,
rep from ★ to end.
Row 3: Purl.
Row 4: ★P3tog, (K1, P1, K1) all into next st,
rep from ★ to end.

These 4 rows form trinity st.
Work in trinity st for a further 12 rows, ending
with a WS row.
Next row (RS): K3 (4: 5: 3: 1), K2tog, ★K8 (5:
8: 6: 5), K2tog, rep from ★ to last 3 (4: 5: 3: 1) sts,
K to end. 43 (45: 47: 49: 51) sts.
Now cont in double moss st as folls:
Row 1 (WS): K1, ★P1, K1, rep from ★ to end.
Row 2: As row 2.
Row 3: P1, ★K1, P1, rep from ★ to end.
Row 4: As row 3.
These 4 rows form double moss st.
Cont in double moss st until back measures
51 (52: 52: 53: 53) cm, ending with a WS row.
Shape armholes
Keeping patt correct, cast off 6 sts at beg of next
2 rows. 31 (33: 35: 37: 39) sts.
Cont straight until armhole measures 24 (24: 25:
25: 26) cm, ending with a WS row.
Shape shoulders
Cast off 4 (4: 5: 5: 5) sts at beg of next 2 rows,
then 4 (5: 5: 5: 6) sts at beg of foll 2 rows.
Break yarn and leave rem 15 (15: 15: 17: 17) sts
on a holder.

POCKET LININGS (make 2)

Cast on 11 sts using 12mm (US 17) needles.
Beg with a K row, work in st st for 15 cm,
ending with a WS row.
Break yarn and leave sts on a holder.

LEFT FRONT

Cast on 28 (32: 32: 32: 36) sts using 12mm
(US 17) needles.
Work in trinity st as given for back for 16 rows,
ending with a WS row.
Next row (RS): K4 (3: 3: 3: 2), K2tog, ★K7 (3:
4: 6: 3), K2tog, rep from ★ to last 4 (2: 3: 3: 2) sts,
K to end. 25 (26: 27: 28: 29) sts.
Now cont in double moss st as folls:
Row 1 (WS): K1 (0: 1: 0: 1), ★P1, K1, rep from
★ to end.
Row 2: ★K1, P1, rep from ★ to last 1 (0: 1: 0: 1) st,
K1 (0: 1: 0: 1).
Row 3: P1 (0: 1: 0: 1), ★K1, P1, rep from ★ to
end.
Row 4: ★P1, K1, rep from ★ to last 1 (0: 1: 0: 1) st,
P1 (0: 1: 0: 1).
These 4 rows form double moss st.
Work in double moss st for a further 5 rows,
ending with a WS row.

Place pocket

Next row (RS): Patt 3 (4: 5: 6: 7) sts, slip next 11 sts onto a holder and, in their place, patt across 11 sts of first pocket lining, patt to end.
Cont in double moss st until left front matches back to beg of armhole shaping, ending with a WS row.

Shape armhole

Keeping patt correct, cast off 6 sts at beg of next row. 19 (20: 21: 22: 23) sts.
Cont straight until left front matches back to start of shoulder shaping, ending with a WS row.

Shape shoulder

Cast off 4 (4: 5: 5: 5) sts at beg of next row, then 4 (5: 5: 5: 6) sts at beg of foll alt row.
Work 1 row, ending with a WS row.
Break yarn and leave rem 11 (11: 11: 12: 12) sts on a holder.

RIGHT FRONT

Cast on 28 (32: 32: 32: 36) sts using 12mm (US 17) needles.
Work in trinity st as given for back for 16 rows, ending with a WS row.
Next row (RS): K4 (3: 3: 3: 2), K2tog, ★K7 (3: 4: 6: 3), K2tog, rep from ★ to last 4 (2: 3: 3: 2) sts, K to end. 25 (26: 27: 28: 29) sts.
Now cont in double moss st as folls:
Row 1 (WS): ★K1, P1, rep from ★ to last 1 (0: 1: 0: 1) st, K1 (0: 1: 0: 1).
Row 2: K1 (0: 1: 0: 1), ★P1, K1, rep from ★ to end.
Row 3: ★P1, K1, rep from ★ to last 1 (0: 1: 0: 1) st, P1 (0: 1: 0: 1).
Row 4: P1 (0: 1: 0: 1), ★K1, P1, rep from ★ to end.
These 4 rows form double moss st.
Work in double moss st for a further 5 rows, ending with a WS row.

Place pocket

Next row (RS): Patt 11 sts, slip next 11 sts onto a holder and, in their place, patt across 11 sts of second pocket lining, patt to end.
Complete to match left front, reversing shapings.

SLEEVES (both alike)

Cast on 36 (36: 36: 40: 40) sts using 12mm (US 17) needles.
Work in trinity st as given for back for 16 rows, ending with a WS row.
Next row (RS): K3 (3: 3: 1: 1), K2tog, ★K5 (5: 5: 4: 4), K2tog, rep from ★ to last 3 (3: 3: 1: 1) sts, K to end. 31 (31: 31: 33: 33) sts.

Beg with row 1, cont in double moss st as given for back, shaping sides by inc 1 st at each end of 4th and foll 8th (8th: 6th: 8th: 6th) row until there are 39 (39: 41: 41: 43) sts, taking inc sts into patt.
Cont straight until sleeve measures 52.5 (52.5: 53.5: 53.5: 53.5) cm, ending with a WS row.
Cast off.

MAKING UP

PRESS as described on the information page. Join both shoulder seams using back stitch, or mattress st if preferred.

Hood

With RS facing and using 12mm (US 17) needles, patt first 10 (10: 10: 11: 11) sts from right front holder, work tog last st from right front holder with first st from back holder, patt next 13 (13: 13: 15: 15) sts from back holder, work tog last st from back holder with first st from left front holder, then patt rem 10 (10: 10: 11: 11) sts from left front holder.
35 (35: 35: 39: 39) sts.
Place marker on centre st.
Keeping double moss st correct as set by fronts, cont as folls:
Work 1 row.
Next row (RS): Patt to marked st, M1, patt marked st, M1, patt to end.
Rep last 2 rows 5 times more.
47 (47: 47: 51: 51) sts.
Cont straight until hood measures 28 (28: 29: 29: 30) cm from pick-up row, ending with a WS row.
Next row (RS): Patt to within 2 sts of marked st, work 2 tog, patt marked st, work 2 tog tbl, patt to end.
Work 1 row.
Working all decreases as set by last row, dec 1 st at either side of marked st on 2nd and foll alt row, then on foll 3 rows, ending with a WS row.
35 (35: 35: 39: 39) sts.
Cast off.
Join top seam of hood.

Pocket tops (both alike)

Slip 11 sts from pocket holder onto 10mm (US 15) needles and rejoin yarn with RS facing.
Work in double moss st as set for 3 rows.
Cast off in patt (on WS).

Belt

Cast on 6 sts using 10mm (US 15) needles.

Row 1 (RS): (K1, P1) 3 times.
Row 2: As row 1.
Row 3: (P1, K1) 3 times.
Row 4: As row 3.
These 4 rows form double moss st.
Cont in double moss st until belt measures 150 cm.
Cast off.
See information page for finishing instructions, setting in sleeves using the square set-in method.

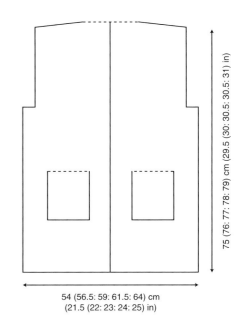

75 (76: 77: 78: 79) cm (29.5 (30: 30.5: 30.5: 31) in)

54 (56.5: 59: 61.5: 64) cm
(21.5 (22: 23: 24: 25) in)

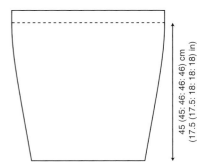

45 (45: 46: 46: 46) cm
(17.5 (17.5: 18: 18: 18) in)

STEEL

KIM HARGREAVES

YARN

	S-M	M-L	L-XL	XL-XXL
To fit	97-102	102-107	107-112	112-117 cm
chest	38-40	40-42	42-44	44-46 in

Rowan Biggy Print

	15	16	18	19 x 100gm

(photographed in Choc Chip 257)

NEEDLES

1 pair 15mm (US 19) needles
1 pair 20mm (US 36) needles

TENSION

5½ sts and 7 rows to 10 cm measured over stocking stitch using 20mm (US 36) needles.

BACK

Cast on 36 (38: 40: 42) sts using 20mm (US 36) needles. Beg with a K row, cont in st st until back measures 40 cm, ending with a WS row.
Shape raglan armholes
Cast off 3 sts at beg of next 2 rows.
30 (32: 34: 36) sts.
Next row (RS): K2, K2tog, K to last 4 sts, K2tog tbl, K2.
Next row: P2, P2tog tbl, P to last 4 sts, P2tog, P2.
26 (28: 30: 32) sts.

Working all decreases as set by last 2 rows, dec 1 st at each end of next 1 (3: 1: 3) rows, then on foll 7 (6: 8: 7) alt rows, then on foll row, ending with a WS row.
Cast off rem 8 (8: 10: 10) sts.

FRONT

Work as given for back until 14 (14: 16: 16) sts rem in raglan shaping.
Work 1 row, ending with a WS row.
Shape front neck
Next row (RS): K1, K2tog tbl and turn, leaving rem sts on a holder.
Work each side of neck separately.
Next row (WS): P2tog and fasten off.
With RS facing, rejoin yarn to rem sts, cast off centre 7 (7: 9: 9) sts (one st on right needle), K2tog, pass 2nd st on right needle over this st (to cast off another st), K rem st on left needle.
Next row (WS): P2tog and fasten off.

SLEEVES

Cast on 20 (20: 22: 22) sts using 20mm (US 36) needles.
Beg with a K row, cont in st st as folls:
Work 10 rows, ending with a WS row.
Next row (RS): K2, M1, K to last 2 sts, M1, K2.
Working all increases as set by last row, inc 1 st at each end of every foll 6th row until there are 28 (28: 30: 30) sts.
Cont straight until sleeve measures 51 (51: 52: 52) cm, ending with a WS row.
Shape raglan
Cast off 3 sts at beg of next 2 rows.
22 (22: 24: 24) sts.
Working all decreases 2 sts in from ends of rows as given for back, dec 1 st at each end of next and every foll 4th row to 16 (16: 18: 18) sts, then on every foll alt row until 12 sts rem.
Work 1 row, ending with a WS row.
Left sleeve only
Dec 1 st at each end of next row. 10 sts.
Cast off 2 sts at beg of next row. 8 sts.
Dec 1 st at beg of next row. 7 sts.
Cast off 3 sts at beg and dec 1 st at end of next row.
Right sleeve only
Cast off 3 sts at beg and dec 1 st at end of next row.
Work 1 row.
Rep last 2 rows once more.
Both sleeves
Cast off rem 3 sts.

MAKING UP

PRESS as described on the information page.
Join both front and right back raglan seams using back stitch, or mattress st if preferred.
Collar
With RS facing and using 15mm (US 19) needles, pick up and knit 6 sts from left sleeve, 12 (12: 14: 14) sts from front, 6 sts from right sleeve, then 8 (8: 10: 10) sts from back.
32 (32: 36: 36) sts.
Beg with a K row, cont in st st until collar measures 10 cm.
Change to 20mm (US 36) needles.
Cont in st st until collar measures 25 cm.
Cast off **loosely**.
See information page for finishing instructions, reversing collar seam for turn-back.

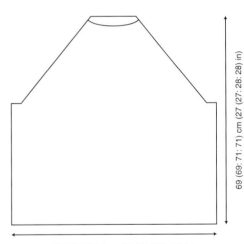

69 (69: 71: 71) cm (27 (27: 28: 28) in)

65.5 (69: 72.5: 76.5) cm (26 (27: 28.5: 30) in)

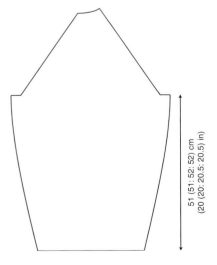

51 (51: 52: 52) cm (20 (20: 20.5: 20.5) in)

TOAST

KIM HARGREAVES

YARN
One size to fit average size adult
Rowan Chunky Print
        2   x   100gm
(photographed in Temper 073)

NEEDLES
1 pair 8mm (no 0) (US 11) needles

TENSION
11 sts and 14 rows to 10 cm measured over flattened rib pattern using 8mm (US 11) needles.

LEG WARMERS (both alike)
Cast on 34 sts using 8mm (US 11) needles.
Row 1 (RS): K2, ★P2, K2, rep from ★ to end.
Row 2: P2, ★K2, P2, rep from ★ to end.
These 2 rows form rib.
Cont in rib until work measures 30 cm, ending with a WS row.
Cast off in rib.

MAKING UP
PRESS as described on the information page.
Join back seam using back stitch or mattresss stitch if preferred.

FLOAT

KIM HARGREAVES

YARN

	XS	S	M	L	XL	
To fit bust	81	86	91	97	102	cm
	32	34	36	38	40	in

Rowan Big Wool
        9   10   10   11   12 x 100gm
(photographed in Ice Blue 021)

NEEDLES
1 pair 10mm (no 000) (US 15) needles
1 pair 12mm (US 17) needles

BUTTONS - 5 x 75326

TENSION
8 sts and 12 rows to 10 cm measured over stocking stitch using 12mm (US 17) needles.

BACK
Cast on 79 (81: 83: 85: 87) sts using 12mm (US 17) needles.
Row 1 (RS): K1, ★P1, K1, rep from ★ to end.
Row 2: As row 1.
These 2 rows form moss st.
Work in moss st for a further 14 rows, ending with a WS row.
Cont in patt as folls:

Row 1 (RS): K2tog, K to last 2 sts, K2tog.
77 (79: 81: 83: 85) sts.
Row 2: P1 (2: 1: 2: 1), ★yrn, P2, then lift the yrn over the last 2 sts and off right needle, P2, rep from ★ to last 0 (1: 0: 1: 0) sts, P0 (1: 0: 1: 0).
Row 3: Knit.
Row 4: P1 (2: 1: 2: 1), ★P2, yrn, P2, then lift the yrn over the last 2 sts and off right needle, rep from ★ to last 4 (1: 4: 1: 4) sts, P4 (1: 4: 1: 4).
These 4 rows form patt and start shaping.
Keeping patt correct, dec 1 st at each end of 3rd and every foll 6th row to 69 (71: 73: 75: 77) sts, then on every foll 4th row to 59 (63: 63: 67: 67) sts, then on foll 5 (7: 6: 8: 7) alt rows, then on foll 3 rows, ending with a WS row.
43 (43: 45: 45: 47) sts.
Shape shoulders and back neck
Cast off 4 (4: 5: 4: 5) sts at beg of next 2 rows.
35 (35: 35: 37: 37) sts.
Next row (RS): Cast off 4 (4: 5: 4: 5) sts, K until there are 8 (8: 7: 8: 7) sts on right needle and turn, leaving rem sts on a holder.
Work each side of neck separately.
Cast off 3 sts at beg of next row.
Cast off rem 5 (5: 4: 5: 4) sts.
With RS facing, rejoin yarn to rem sts, cast off centre 11 (11: 11: 13: 13) sts, K to end.
Complete to match first side, reversing shapings.

LEFT FRONT
Cast on 45 (46: 47: 48: 49) sts using 12mm (US 17) needles.
Row 1 (RS): ★K1, P1, rep from ★ to last 1 (0: 1: 0: 1) st, K1 (0: 1: 0: 1).
Row 2: K1 (0: 1: 0: 1), ★P1, K1, rep from ★ to end.
These 2 rows form moss st.
Work in moss st for a further 13 rows, ending with a RS row.
Row 16 (WS): Moss st 6 sts and slip these sts onto a holder, M1, moss st to end.
40 (41: 42: 43: 44) sts.
Cont in patt as folls:
Row 1 (RS): K2tog, K to end.
39 (40: 41: 42: 43) sts.
Row 2: P3 (3: 1: 1: 3), ★yrn, P2, then lift the yrn over the last 2 sts and off right needle, P2, rep from ★ to last 0 (1: 0: 1: 0) sts, P0 (1: 0: 1: 0).
These 2 rows set position of patt as given for back.
Keeping patt correct, cont as folls:

Divide for opening

Next row (RS): Patt to last 19 sts and turn, leaving rem 19 sts on a holder.

Work on this set of 20 (21: 22: 23: 24) sts only for side front.

Dec 1 st at beg of 4th and every foll 6th row until 17 (18: 19: 20: 21) sts rem.

Work 3 rows, ending with a WS row.

Break yarn and leave sts on a second holder.

With RS facing, rejoin yarn to 19 sts from first holder and patt 20 rows for centre front section, ending with a WS row.

Break yarn.

Join sections

Next row (RS): Patt 17 (18: 19: 20: 21) sts of side front, then patt 19 sts of centre front. 36 (37: 38: 39: 40) sts.

Work 1 row, ending with a WS row.

Dec 1 st at beg of next and every foll 4th row to 30 (32: 32: 34: 34) sts, then on foll 2 (4: 3: 5: 4) alt rows. 28 (28: 29: 29: 30) sts.

Work 1 row, ending with a WS row.

Shape neck

Next row (RS): K2tog, K23 (23: 24: 23: 24) and turn, leaving last 3 (3: 3: 4: 4) sts on a holder.

Dec 1 st at side edge of 2nd and foll alt row, then on foll 3 rows **and at same time** dec 1 st at neck edge of next 4 rows, then on foll alt row. 14 (14: 15: 14: 15) sts.

Shape shoulder

Cast off 4 (4: 5: 4: 5) sts at beg and dec 1 st at end of next row.

Work 1 row.

Cast off 4 (4: 5: 4: 5) sts at beg of next row.

Work 1 row.

Cast off rem 5 (5: 4: 5: 4) sts.

RIGHT FRONT

Cast on 45 (46: 47: 48: 49) sts using 12mm (US 17) needles.

Row 1 (RS): K1 (0: 1: 0: 1), ★P1, K1, rep from ★ to end.

Row 2: ★K1, P1, rep from ★ to last 1 (0: 1: 0: 1) st, K1 (0: 1: 0: 1).

These 2 rows form moss st.

Work in moss st for a further 13 rows, ending with a RS row.

Row 16 (WS): Moss st to last 6 sts, M1 and turn, leaving last 6 sts on a holder. 40 (41: 42: 43: 44) sts.

Cont in patt as folls:

Row 1 (RS): K to last 2 sts, K2tog. 39 (40: 41: 42: 43) sts.

Row 2: P1 (2: 1: 2: 1), ★yrn, P2, then lift the yrn over the last 2 sts and off right needle, P2, rep from ★ to last 2 (2: 0: 0: 2) sts, P2 (2: 0: 0: 2).

These 2 rows set position of patt as given for back.

Keeping patt correct, cont as folls:

Divide for opening

Next row (RS): Patt 19 sts and turn, leaving rem 20 (21: 22: 23: 24) sts on a holder.

Work a further 19 rows on these sts for centre front section, ending with a WS row.

Break yarn and leave sts on a second holder.

With RS facing, rejoin yarn to 20 (21: 22: 23: 24) sts from first holder and work side front as folls:

Dec 1 st at end of 4th and every foll 6th row until 17 (18: 19: 20: 21) sts rem.

Work 3 rows, ending with a WS row.

Break yarn.

Join sections

Next row (RS): Patt 19 sts of centre front, then patt 17 (18: 19: 20: 21) sts of side front. 36 (37: 38: 39: 40) sts.

Work 1 row, ending with a WS row.

Dec 1 st at end of next and every foll 4th row to 30 (32: 32: 34: 34) sts, then on foll 2 (4: 3: 5: 4) alt rows. 28 (28: 29: 29: 30) sts.

Complete to match left front, reversing shapings.

MAKING UP

PRESS as described on the information page. Join both shoulder seams using back stitch, or mattress st if preferred.

Button band

Slip 6 sts from left front holder onto 10mm (US 15) needles and rejoin yarn with RS facing.

Cont in moss st as set until band, when slightly stretched, fits up left front opening edge to neck shaping, ending with a WS row.

Break yarn and leave sts on a holder.

Slip stitch band in place.

Mark positions for 5 buttons on this band – first to come just above moss st border, last to come just below neck shaping and rem 3 buttons evenly spaced between.

Buttonhole band

Slip 6 sts from right front holder onto 10mm (US 15) needles and rejoin yarn with WS facing.

Complete as given for button band, with the addition of 5 buttonholes worked to correspond with positions marked for buttons as folls:

Buttonhole row (RS): Moss st 1 st, work 2 tog, (yrn) twice (to make a buttonhole – on foll row work twice into this double loop), work 2 tog tbl, moss st 1 st.

Slip stitch band in place.

Collar

With RS facing and using 10mm (US 15) needles, slip 6 sts of buttonhole band and then 3 (3: 3: 4: 4) sts from right front holder onto right needle, rejoin yarn and pick up and knit 9 sts up right side of neck, 16 (16: 16: 18: 18) sts from back, and 9 sts down left side of neck, then K 3 (3: 3: 4: 4) sts from left front holder, and moss st 6 sts from button band. 52 (52: 52: 56: 56) sts.

Row 1 (RS of collar, WS of body): Moss st 5 sts, K2, ★P2, K2, rep from ★ to last 5 sts, moss st 5 sts.

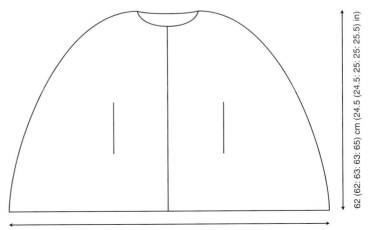

62 (62: 63: 63: 65) cm (24.5 (24.5: 25: 25: 25.5) in)

99 (101.5: 104: 106.5: 109) cm (39 (40: 41: 42: 43) in)

Row 2: Moss st 5 sts, P2, ★K2, P2, rep from ★ to last 5 sts, moss st 5 sts.
Rep these 2 rows until collar measures 25 cm.
Cast off in patt.
Side front pocket edgings (both alike)
With RS facing and using 10mm (US 15)

needles, pick up and knit 15 sts along side front edge of opening.
Work in moss st as given for back for 4 rows.
Cast off in moss st (on WS).
Centre front pocket edgings (both alike)
With RS facing and using 10mm (US 15)

needles, pick up and knit 14 sts along centre front edge of opening.
Cast off knitwise (on WS).
Lay side front pocket edging over centre front and neatly stitch ends of all pocket edgings in place.
See information page for finishing instructions.

Design number 10

MAJOR

KIM HARGREAVES

YARN

	S	M	L	XL	XXL	
To fit chest	97	102	107	112	117	cm
	38	40	42	44	46	in

Rowan Big Wool

| | 10 | 10 | 11 | 12 | 13 | x 100gm |

(photographed in Camouflage 023)

NEEDLES

1 pair 10mm (no 000) (US 15) needles
1 pair 12mm (US 17) needles

BUTTONS

11 x 75334

TENSION

8 sts and 12 rows to 10 cm measured over stocking stitch using 12mm (US 17) needles.

BACK

Cast on 48 (50: 52: 54: 56) sts using 10mm (US 15) needles.
Row 1 (RS): K0 (0: 1: 0: 0), P1 (2: 2: 0: 1), ★K2, P2, rep from ★ to last 3 (0: 1: 2: 3) sts, K2 (0: 1: 2: 2), P1 (0: 0: 0: 1).
Row 2: P0 (0: 1: 0: 0), K1 (2: 2: 0: 1), ★P2, K2, rep from ★ to last 3 (0: 1: 2: 3) sts, P2 (0: 1: 2: 2), K1 (0: 0: 0: 1).
These 2 rows form rib.
Work in rib for a further 8 rows, ending with a WS row.
Change to 12mm (US 17) needles.
Beg with a K row, cont in st st until back measures 37 (37: 38: 38: 39) cm, ending with a WS row.
Shape armholes
Cast off 4 sts at beg of next 2 rows.
40 (42: 44: 46: 48) sts.
Dec 1 st at each end of next 3 (3: 4: 4: 5) rows.
34 (36: 36: 38: 38) sts.
Cont straight until armhole measures 23 (24: 24: 25: 25) cm, ending with a WS row.
Shape shoulders and back neck
Cast off 3 (4: 4: 4: 4) sts at beg of next 2 rows.
28 (28: 28: 30: 30) sts.
Next row (RS): Cast off 3 (4: 4: 4: 4) sts, K until there are 7 (6: 6: 6: 6) sts on right needle and turn, leaving rem sts on a holder.
Work each side of neck separately.
Cast off 3 sts at beg of next row.
Cast off rem 4 (3: 3: 3: 3) sts.
With RS facing, rejoin yarn to rem sts, cast off centre 8 (8: 8: 10: 10) sts, K to end.
Complete to match first side, reversing shapings.

PATCH POCKETS (make 2)

Cast on 14 sts using 10mm (US 15) needles.
Rows 1 to 4: Purl.
Row 5 (WS of pocket): Purl.
Row 6: P1, K12, P1.
Rows 7 to 18: As rows 5 and 6, 6 times.
Break yarn and leave sts on a holder.

LEFT FRONT

Cast on 6 sts using 10mm (US 15) needles.
Break yarn, leaving these sts on needle.
Onto same needle, cast on a further 5 (6: 7: 8: 9) sts using 10mm (US 15) needles.
Join sections
Next row (RS): K0 (0: 1: 0: 0), P1 (2: 2: 0: 1), (K2, P2) 1 (1: 1: 2: 2) times, with **WS** of pocket facing knit across all 14 sts of pocket, then, with RS facing, work across rem 6 cast-on sts as folls: P2, K2, P2.
25 (26: 27: 28: 29) sts.
Next row: K2, P2, K2, P14, (K2, P2) 1 (1: 1: 2: 2) times, K1 (2: 2: 0: 1), P0 (0: 1: 0: 0).
Next row: K0 (0: 1: 0: 0), P1 (2: 2: 0: 1), (K2, P2) 1 (1: 1: 2: 2) times, K14, P2, K2, P2.
Rep last 2 rows 3 times more, then first of these 2 rows again, ending with a WS row.
Change to 12mm (US 17) needles.
Beg with a K row, cont in st st until left front matches back to beg of armhole shaping, ending with a WS row.
Shape armhole
Cast off 4 sts at beg of next row.
21 (22: 23: 24: 25) sts.
Work 1 row.
Dec 1 st at armhole edge of next 3 (3: 4: 4: 5) rows.
18 (19: 19: 20: 20) sts.
Cont straight until 7 rows less have been worked than on back to start of shoulder shaping, ending with a RS row.
Shape neck
Cast off 4 (4: 4: 5: 5) sts at beg of next row.
14 (15: 15: 15: 15) sts.
Dec 1 st at neck edge of next 3 rows, then on foll alt row. 10 (11: 11: 11: 11) sts.
Work 1 row, ending with a WS row.
Shape shoulder
Cast off 3 (4: 4: 4: 4) sts at beg of next and foll alt row.
Work 1 row.
Cast off rem 4 (3: 3: 3: 3) sts.

RIGHT FRONT

Cast on 5 (6: 7: 8: 9) sts using 10mm (US 15) needles.

Break yarn, leaving these sts on needle.

Onto same needle, cast on a further 6 sts using 10mm (US 15) needles.

Join sections

Next row (RS): P2, K2, P2, with **WS** of pocket facing knit across all 14 sts of pocket, then, with RS facing, work across rem 5 (6: 7: 8: 9) cast-on sts as folls: (P2, K2) 1 (1: 1: 2: 2) times, P1 (2: 2: 0: 1), K0 (0: 1: 0: 0). 25 (26: 27: 28: 29) sts.

Next row: P0 (0: 1: 0: 0), K1 (2: 2: 0: 1), (P2, K2) 1 (1: 1: 2: 2) times, P14, K2, P2, K2.

Next row: P2, K2, P2, K14, (P2, K2) 1 (1: 1: 2: 2) times, P1 (2: 2: 0: 1), K0 (0: 1: 0: 0).

Rep last 2 rows 3 times more, then first of these 2 rows again, ending with a WS row.

Change to 12mm (US 17) needles and complete to match left front, reversing shapings.

SLEEVES (both alike)

Cast on 28 (28: 30: 30: 30) sts using 10mm (US 15) needles.

Row 1 (RS): K1 (1: 2: 2: 2), *P2, K2, rep from * to last 3 (3: 4: 4: 4) sts, P2, K1 (1: 2: 2: 2).

Row 2: P1 (1: 2: 2: 2), *K2, P2, rep from * to last 3 (3: 4: 4: 4) sts, K2, P1 (1: 2: 2: 2).

These 2 rows form rib.

Work in rib for a further 8 rows, ending with a WS row.

Change to 12mm (US 17) needles.

Beg with a K row, cont in st st, shaping sides by inc 1 st at each end of 11th and foll 22nd row. 32 (32: 34: 34: 34) sts.

Cont straight until sleeve measures 49 (50: 50: 51: 51) cm, ending with a WS row.

Shape top

Cast off 4 sts at beg of next 2 rows. 24 (24: 26: 26: 26) sts.

Dec 1 st at each end of 3rd and every foll 4th row until 18 (18: 20: 20: 20) sts rem.

Work 1 row.

Dec 1 st at each end of next and every foll alt row to 12 sts, then on foll row, ending with a WS row. Cast off rem 10 sts.

MAKING UP

PRESS as described on the information page.

Join both shoulder seams using back stitch, or mattress st if preferred.

Button band

With RS facing and using 10mm (US 15) needles, pick up and knit 48 sts up right front opening edge, between cast-on edge and neck shaping.

Row 1 (WS): K1, *P2, K2, rep from * to last 3 sts, P2, K1.

Row 2: K3, *P2, K2, rep from * to last st, K1.

These 2 rows form rib.

Work in rib for a further 5 rows.

Cast off in rib.

Buttonhole band

Work as given for button band, picking up sts down left front opening edge and with the addition of 5 buttonholes worked in row 5 as folls:

Row 5 (buttonhole row) (WS): Rib 3, *yrn (to make a buttonhole), work 2 tog, rib 8, rep from * to last 5 sts, yrn (to make 5th buttonhole), work 2 tog, rib 3.

Collar

Cast on 46 (46: 46: 50: 50) sts using 10mm (US 15) needles.

Row 1 (RS): K2, *P2, K2, rep from * to end.

Row 2: K1, P1, *K2, P2, rep from * to last 4 sts, K2, P1, K1.

These 2 rows form rib.

Cont in rib until collar measures 12 cm.

Cast off in rib.

Positioning ends of collar halfway across top of bands, sew cast-on edge of collar to neck edge.

Pocket flaps (make 2)

Cast on 16 sts using 10mm (US 15) needles.

Beg with row 2, work in rib as given for button band for 4 rows, ending with a WS row.

Row 5 (RS): K2, K2tog tbl, yrn (to make a buttonhole), rib to last 4 sts, yrn (to make 2nd buttonhole), K2tog, K2.

Cont in rib until pocket flap measures 10 cm.

Cast off in rib.

Fold pockets up onto RS of fronts, folding level with cast-on edge of side sections, and stitch in place. Position pocket flap above pocket opening using photograph as a guide and stitch in place. Attach buttons to pockets to correspond with buttonholes in flaps.

Epaulettes (make 2)

Cast on 10 sts using 10mm (US 15) needles.

Row 1 (RS): K2, *P2, K2, rep from * to end.

Row 2: P2, *K2, P2, rep from * to end.

These 2 rows form rib.

Cont in rib until epaulette measures 5 cm.

Cast off in rib.

Lay epaulette over shoulder seam, matching one short end to armhole edge, and stitch these armhole edges together. Secure other end of epaulette to shoulder seam by attaching a button through all layers.

See information page for finishing instructions, setting in sleeves using the set-in method.

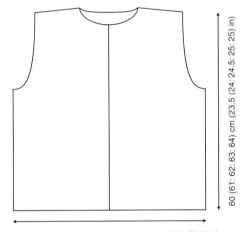

60 (62.5: 65: 67.5: 70) cm (23.5 (24.5: 25.5: 26.5: 27.5) in)

60 (61: 62: 63: 64) cm (23.5 (24: 24.5: 25: 25) in)

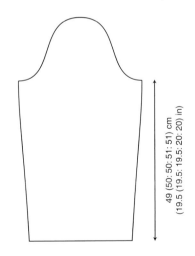

49 (50: 50: 51: 51) cm (19.5 (19.5: 19.5: 20: 20) in)

SWEEP

KIM HARGREAVES

YARN

	XS-S	S-M	M-L	L-XL	
To fit bust	81-86	86-91	91-97	97-102	cm
	32-34	34-36	36-38	38-40	in

Rowan Biggy Print and Chunky Print

A Biggy Print	Glum	244			
	9	9	10	11	x 100gm
B Chunky Print	Temper	073			
	3	3	4	4	x 100gm

NEEDLES

1 pair 20mm (US 36) needles

TENSION

5½ sts and 7 rows to 10 cm measured over striped stocking stitch using 20mm (US 36) needles.

BACK

Cast on 29 (31: 33: 35) sts using 20mm (US 36) needles and yarn A.
Beg with a K row, work in st st as folls:
Using yarn A, work 2 rows.
Join in yarn B.
Using yarn B, work 2 rows.
Last 4 rows form striped st st.
Cont in striped st st until back measures 72 cm, ending with a WS row.

Shape armholes

Keeping stripes correct, cast off 3 sts at beg of next 2 rows. 23 (25: 27: 29) sts.
Cont straight until armhole measures 24 (25: 26: 27) cm, ending with a WS row.

Shape shoulders and back neck

Next row (RS): Cast off 3 (4: 4: 4) sts, K until there are 6 (6: 6: 7) sts on right needle and turn, leaving rem sts on a holder.
Work each side of neck separately.
Cast off 2 sts at beg of next row.
Cast off rem 4 (4: 4: 5) sts.
With RS facing, rejoin appropriate yarn to rem sts, cast off centre 5 (5: 7: 7) sts, K to end.
Complete to match first side, reversing shapings.

LEFT FRONT

Cast on 15 (16: 17: 18) sts using 20mm (US 36) needles and yarn A.
Beg with a K row and 2 rows using yarn A, cont in striped st st as given for back as folls:
Cont straight until left front matches back to beg of armhole shaping, ending with a WS row.

Shape armhole

Keeping stripes correct, cast off 3 sts at beg of next row. 12 (13: 14: 15) sts.
Cont straight until 5 rows less have been worked than on back to start of shoulder shaping, ending with a RS row.

Shape neck

Next row (RS): P3 (3: 4: 4) and slip these sts onto a holder, P to end. 9 (10: 10: 11) sts.
Dec 1 st at neck edge of next 2 rows. 7 (8: 8: 9) sts.
Work 2 rows, ending with a WS row.

Shape shoulder

Cast off 3 (4: 4: 4) sts at beg of next row.
Work 1 row. Cast off rem 4 (4: 4: 5) sts.

RIGHT FRONT

Work to match left front, reversing shapings.

SLEEVES (both alike)

Cast on 19 (21: 21: 23) sts using 20mm (US 36) needles and yarn A.
Beg with a K row and 2 rows using yarn A, cont in striped st st as given for back, shaping sides by inc 1 st at each end of 9th and every foll 6th row until there are 27 (29: 29: 31) sts.
Cont straight until sleeve measures 48.5 (48.5: 49.5: 49.5) cm, ending with a WS row.
Cast off **loosely**.

MAKING UP

PRESS as described on the information page. Join both shoulder seams using back stitch, or mattress st if preferred.

Neckband

With RS facing, using 20mm (US 36) needles and yarn A, slip 3 (3: 4: 4) sts from right front holder onto right needle, rejoin yarn and pick up and knit 5 sts up right side of neck, 9 (9: 11: 11) sts from back, and 5 sts down left side of neck, then K 3 (3: 4: 4) sts from left front holder. 25 (25: 29: 29) sts.
Cast off knitwise (on WS).

Front bands (both alike)

With RS facing, using 20mm (US 36) needles and yarn A, pick up and knit 50 (51: 51: 52) sts evenly along front opening edge, between cast-on edge and top of neckband.
Cast off knitwise (on WS).
See information page for finishing instructions, setting in sleeves using the square set-in method.

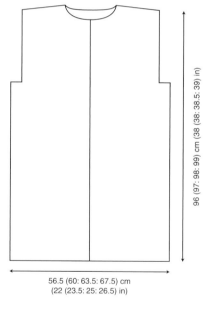

56.5 (60: 63.5: 67.5) cm
(22 (23.5: 25: 26.5) in)

96 (97: 98: 99) cm (38 (38: 38.5: 39) in)

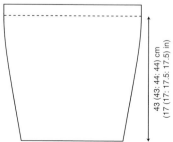

43 (43: 44: 44) cm
(17 (17: 17.5: 17.5) in)

MOLTEN

KIM HARGREAVES

YARN

	XS-S	S-M	M-L	L-XL	
To fit bust	81-86	86-91	91-97	97-102	cm
	32-34	34-36	36-38	38-40	in

Rowan Biggy Print and Chunky Print

A Biggy Print	Sheep	258			
	7	8	9	10	x 100gm
B Chunky Print	Woolly	071			
	3	3	4	4	x 100gm

NEEDLES

1 pair 20mm (US 36) needles

TENSION

5½ sts and 7 rows to 10 cm measured over striped stocking stitch using 20mm (US 36) needles.

BACK

Cast on 31 (33: 35: 37) sts using 20mm (US 36) needles and yarn A.
Beg with a K row, work in st st as folls:
Using yarn A, work 2 rows.
Join in yarn B.
Using yarn B, work 2 rows.
Last 4 rows form striped st st.
Cont in striped st st until back measures 46 cm, ending with a WS row.

Shape armholes

Keeping stripes correct, cast off 3 sts at beg of next 2 rows.
25 (27: 29: 31) sts.
Cont straight until armhole measures 25 (26: 27: 28) cm, ending with a WS row.

Shape shoulders and back neck

Next row (RS): Cast off 3 (4: 4: 4) sts, K until there are 7 (7: 7: 8) sts on right needle and turn, leaving rem sts on a holder.
Work each side of neck separately.
Cast off 3 sts at beg of next row.
Cast off rem 4 (4: 4: 5) sts.
With RS facing, rejoin appropriate yarn to rem sts, cast off centre 5 (5: 7: 7) sts, K to end.
Complete to match first side, reversing shapings.

FRONT

Work as given for back until 4 rows less have been worked than on back to start of back neck shaping, ending with a WS row.

Shape front neck

Next row (RS): K9 (10: 10: 11) and turn, leaving rem sts on a holder.
Work each side of neck separately.
Dec 1 st at neck edge of next 2 rows.
7 (8: 8: 9) sts.
Work 1 row, ending with a WS row.

Shape shoulder

Cast off 3 (4: 4: 4) sts at beg of next row.
Work 1 row.
Cast off rem 4 (4: 4: 5) sts.
With RS facing, rejoin yarn to rem sts, cast off centre 7 (7: 9: 9) sts, K to end.
Complete to match first side, reversing shapings.

SLEEVES (both alike)

Cast on 20 (20: 22: 22) sts using 20mm (US 36) needles and yarn A.
Beg with a K row and 2 rows using yarn A, cont in striped st st as given for back, shaping sides by inc 1 st at each end of 9th and every foll 6th row until there are 28 (28: 30: 30) sts.
Cont straight until sleeve measures 48.5 (48.5: 49.5: 49.5) cm, ending with a WS row.
Cast off **loosely**.

MAKING UP

PRESS as described on the information page.
Join right shoulder seam using back stitch, or mattress st if preferred.

Neckband

With RS facing, using 20mm (US 36) needles and yarn A, pick up and knit 6 sts down left side of neck, 7 (7: 9: 9) sts from front, 6 sts up right side of neck, then 11 (11: 13: 13) sts from back.
30 (30: 34: 34) sts.
Cast off knitwise (on WS).
See information page for finishing instructions, setting in sleeves using the square set-in method.

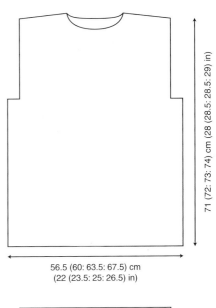

71 (72: 73: 74) cm (28 (28.5: 28.5: 29) in)

56.5 (60: 63.5: 67.5) cm (22 (23.5: 25: 26.5) in)

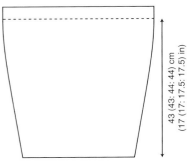

43 (43: 44: 44) cm (17 (17: 17.5: 17.5) in)

HALLE

KIM HARGREAVES

YARN

	XS	S	M	L	XL	
To fit bust	81	86	91	97	102	cm
	32	34	36	38	40	in

Rowan Big Wool
Short version

		XS	S	M	L	XL	
A Wild Berry	025	3	3	4	5	5	x100gm
B Pistachio	029	1	1	1	1	1	x100gm
Long version		5	5	6	6	7	x100gm

(photographed in Bohemian 028)

NEEDLES

1 pair 10mm (no 000) (US 15) needles
1 pair 12mm (US 17) needles

Short version only: 6.00mm (no 4) (US J10) crochet hook for flower trim

TENSION

8 sts and 12 rows to 10 cm measured over stocking stitch using 12mm (US 17) needles.

Pattern note: As row end edges form actual finished armhole edges of garment, it is important these edges are kept neat. Therefore avoid joining in new balls of yarn at these edges.

Short version

BACK

Cast on 30 (32: 34: 36: 38) sts using 10mm (US 15) needles and yarn B.
Break off yarn B and join in yarn A.
Row 1 (RS): K0 (1: 0: 0: 0), P2 (2: 0: 1: 2), *K2, P2, rep from * to last 0 (1: 2: 3: 0) sts, K0 (1: 2: 2: 0), P0 (0: 0: 1: 0).
Row 2: P0 (1: 0: 0: 0), K2 (2: 0: 1: 2), *P2, K2, rep from * to last 0 (1: 2: 3: 0) sts, P0 (1: 2: 2: 0), K0 (0: 0: 1: 0).
These 2 rows form rib.
Work in rib for a further 8 rows, ending with a WS row.
Change to 12mm (US 17) needles.
Beg with a K row, cont in st st as folls:
Work 2 rows.
Join in yarn B.
Row 3 (RS): Using yarn B, K2, M1, K to last 2 sts, M1, K2.
Row 4: Using yarn B, purl.
Break off yarn B and cont using yarn A only.
Working all side seam increases as set by row 3, cont in st st, shaping side seams by inc 1 st at each end of 5th and foll 6th row. 36 (38: 40: 42: 44) sts.
Cont straight until back measures 26 (27: 27: 28: 28) cm, ending with a WS row.

Shape armholes

Cast off 3 sts at beg of next row.
33 (35: 37: 39: 41) sts.
Next row (WS): Cast off 3 sts, K until there are 3 sts on right needle, P to last 3 sts, K3.
30 (32: 34: 36: 38) sts.
Next row: K3, K2tog, K to last 5 sts, K2tog tbl, K3.
Next row: K3, P to last 3 sts, K3.
Rep last 2 rows 1 (1: 2: 2: 3) times more.
26 (28: 28: 30: 30) sts.
Next row (RS): Knit.
Next row: K3, P to last 3 sts, K3.
These 2 rows set the sts – armhole edge 3 sts in garter st with centre sts in st st.
Keeping sts correct as set, cont straight until armhole measures 20 (20: 21: 21: 22) cm, ending with a WS row.

Shape shoulders and back neck

Next row (RS): Cast off 2 (3: 3: 3: 3) sts, K until there are 6 sts on right needle and turn, leaving rem sts on a holder.
Work each side of neck separately.
Cast off 3 sts at beg of next row.
Cast off rem 3 sts.
With RS facing, rejoin yarn to rem sts, cast off centre 10 (10: 10: 12: 12) sts, K to end.
Complete to match first side, reversing shapings.

Long version

BACK

Cast on 40 (42: 44: 46: 48) sts using 10mm (US 15) needles.
Row 1 (RS): K0 (0: 1: 0: 0), P1 (2: 2: 0: 1), *K2, P2, rep from * to last 3 (0: 1: 2: 3) sts, K2 (0: 1: 2: 2), P1 (0: 0: 0: 1).
Row 2: P0 (0: 1: 0: 0), K1 (2: 2: 0: 1), *P2, K2, rep from * to last 3 (0: 1: 2: 3) sts, P2 (0: 1: 2: 2), K1 (0: 0: 0: 1).
These 2 rows form rib.
Work in rib for a further 8 rows, ending with a WS row.
Change to 12mm (US 17) needles.
Beg with a K row, cont in st st as folls:
Work 14 rows.
Next row (RS): K1, K2tog, K to last 3 sts, K2tog tbl, K1.
Working all decreases as set by last row, dec 1 st at each end of every foll 4th row until 30 (32: 34: 36: 38) sts rem.
Work 7 rows, ending with a WS row.

Next row (RS): K2, M1, K to last 2 sts; M1, K2.

Working all increases as set by last row, inc 1 st at each end of every foll 6th row until there are 36 (38: 40: 42: 44) sts.

Cont straight until back measures 64 (65: 65: 66: 66) cm, ending with a WS row.

Complete as given for back of short version from beg of armhole shaping.

Both versions

FRONT

Work as given for back until 8 rows less have been worked than on back to start of shoulder shaping, ending with a WS row.

Shape front neck

Next row (RS): K8 (9: 9: 9: 9) and turn, leaving rem sts on a holder.

Work each side of neck separately.

Dec 1 st at neck edge of next 2 rows, then on foll alt row. 5 (6: 6: 6: 6) sts.

Work 3 rows, ending with a WS row.

Shape shoulder

Cast off 2 (3: 3: 3: 3) sts at beg of next row.

Work 1 row.

Cast off rem 3 sts.

With RS facing, rejoin yarn to rem sts, cast off centre 10 (10: 10: 12: 12) sts, K to end.

Complete to match first side, reversing shapings.

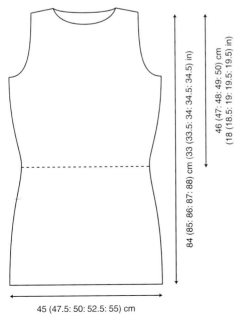

45 (47.5: 50: 52.5: 55) cm
(17.5 (18.5: 19.5: 20.5: 21.5) in)

84 (85: 86: 87: 88) cm (33 (33.5: 34: 34.5: 34.5) in)

46 (47: 48: 49: 50) cm
(18 (18.5: 19: 19.5: 19.5) in)

MAKING UP

PRESS as described on the information page. Join right shoulder seam using back stitch.

Neckband

With RS facing, using 10mm (US 15) needles and yarn A for short version, pick up and knit 8 sts down left side of front neck, 10 (10: 10: 12: 12) sts from front, 8 sts up right side of front neck, then 16 (16: 16: 18: 18) sts from back. 42 (42: 42: 46: 46) sts.

DESIGN NUMBER 14

BLOOM

KIM HARGREAVES

YARN

Rowan Big Wool or Chunky Print

1 x 100gm

(photographed in Big Wool in Lucky 020, in Big Wool in Wild Berry 025 and Pistachio 029 with Halle, and in Chunky Print in Deep End 076 with Violet)

HOOK

6.00mm (no 4) (US J10) crochet hook

FINISHED SIZE

Completed flower is approx 8 cm (3¼ ins) in diameter.

Row 1 (WS): P2, ★K2, P2, rep from ★ to end.
Row 2: K2, ★P2, K2, rep from ★ to end.
Row 3: As row 1.
Cast off in rib.
Join left shoulder and neckband seam.
See information page for finishing instructions.

Short version only

Make and attach flower and streamers (see below), using yarn B for first round of petals and yarn A for all rem sections.

CROCHET ABBREVIATIONS

Ch = chain; **ss** = slip stitch; **dc** = double crochet.

FLOWER

Using 6.00mm (US J10) hook, make 3 ch and join with a ss to form a ring.

Round 1: 1 ch (does NOT count as st), 9 dc into ring, ss to first dc.

(For two colour flower, change to colour for inner petals here.)

Round 2: Working into **front loops only** of dc of previous round, cont as folls: (5 ch, ss into dc at base of 5 ch, ss into next dc) 8 times, 5 ch, ss into dc at base of 5 ch.

(For two colour flower, change to colour for outer petals here.)

Round 3: Working into **back loops only** of dc of round 1, cont as folls: ss into next dc, (8 ch, ss into dc at base of 8 ch, ss into next dc) 8 times, 8 ch, ss into dc at base of 8 ch.

Fasten off.

STREAMERS

First streamer

Using 6.00mm hook, attach yarn to back of flower and make 35 ch.

Fasten off.

Second streamer

Using 6.00mm hook, attach yarn to back of flower and make 30 ch.

Fasten off.

Third streamer

Using 6.00mm hook, attach yarn to back of flower and make 25 ch.

Fasten off.

MAKING UP

DO NOT PRESS.

BUBBLES

KIM HARGREAVES

YARN

	XS	S	M	L	XL	
To fit bust	81	86	91	97	102	cm
	32	34	36	38	40	in

Rowan Big Wool

6 6 7 8 8 x 100gm

(photographed in Pistachio 029)

NEEDLES

1 pair 10mm (no 000) (US 15) needles
1 pair 12mm (US 17) needles

TENSION

8 sts and 12 rows to 10 cm measured over
stocking stitch using 12mm (US 17) needles.

BACK

Cast on 32 (34: 36: 38: 40) sts using 10mm
(US 15) needles.
Row 1 (RS): K0 (0: 1: 0: 0), P1 (2: 2: 0: 1), *K2,
P2, rep from * to last 3 (0: 1: 2: 3) sts, K2 (0: 1:
2: 2), P1 (0: 0: 0: 1).
Row 2: P0 (0: 1: 0: 0), K1 (2: 2: 0: 1), *P2, K2,
rep from * to last 3 (0: 1: 2: 3) sts, P2 (0: 1: 2: 2),
K1 (0: 0: 0: 1).
These 2 rows form rib. Work in rib for a further
6 rows, ending with a WS row.

Change to 12mm (US 17) needles.
Beg with a K row, cont in st st as folls:
Work 2 rows.
Next row (eyelet row) (RS): K3 (4: 5: 6: 2),
*yfwd, K2tog, K3, rep from * to last 4 (5: 6: 7:
3) sts, yfwd, K2tog, K to end.
Cont in st st, shaping side seams by inc 1 st at
each end of 2nd and foll 10th row.
36 (38: 40: 42: 44) sts.
Cont straight until back measures 28 cm, ending
with a WS row.
Shape raglan armholes
Cast off 3 sts at beg of next 2 rows.
30 (32: 34: 36: 38) sts.
Extra small size only
Next row (RS): P1, K2tog, K to last 3 sts,
K2tog tbl, P1. 28 sts.
Next row: K1, P to last st, K1.
Next row: P1, K to last st, P1.
Next row: K1, P to last st, K1.
All sizes
Next row (RS): P1, K2tog, K to last 3 sts,
K2tog tbl, P1.
Next row: K1, P to last st, K1.
Rep last 2 rows 8 (10: 11: 11: 12) times more.
Cast off rem 10 (10: 10: 12: 12) sts.

FRONT

Work as given for back until 16 (16: 16: 18: 18) sts
rem in raglan shaping.
Work 1 row, ending with a WS row.
Shape front neck
Next row (RS): P1, K2tog, K2 and turn,
leaving rem sts on a holder.
Work each side of neck separately.

Next row: P2tog, P1, K1.
Next row: P1, K2tog.
Next row: K2tog and fasten off.
With RS facing, rejoin yarn to rem sts, cast off
centre 6 (6: 6: 8: 8) sts (one st on right needle),
K1, K2tog tbl, P1.
Next row: K1, P1, P2tog tbl.
Next row: K2tog tbl, P1.
Next row: K2tog and fasten off.

SLEEVES

Cast on 24 (24: 26: 26: 28) sts using 10mm
(US 15) needles.
Row 1 (RS): K0 (0: 0: 0: 1), P1 (1: 2: 2: 2), *K2,
P2, rep from * to last 3 (3: 0: 0: 1) sts, K2 (2: 0:
0: 1), P1 (1: 0: 0: 0).
Row 2: P0 (0: 0: 0: 1), K1 (1: 2: 2: 2), *P2, K2,
rep from * to last 3 (3: 0: 0: 1) sts, P2 (2: 0: 0: 1),
K1 (1: 0: 0: 0).
These 2 rows form rib.
Work in rib for a further 8 rows, ending with a
WS row.
Change to 12mm (US 17) needles.
Beg with a K row, cont in st st as folls:
Work 2 rows.
Next row (RS): K2, M1, K to last 2 sts, M1,
K2.
Working all increases as set by last row, inc 1 st
at each end of 8th and foll 8th row, then on
every foll 6th row until there are
36 (36: 38: 38: 40) sts.
Cont straight until sleeve measures 46 (46: 47:
47: 47) cm, ending with a WS row.
Shape raglan
Cast off 3 sts at beg of next 2 rows.

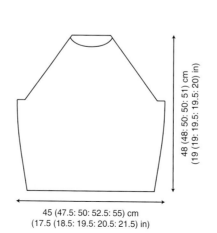

45 (47.5: 50: 52.5: 55) cm
(17.5 (18.5: 19.5: 20.5: 21.5) in)

48 (48: 50: 50: 51) cm
(19 (19: 19.5: 19.5: 20) in)

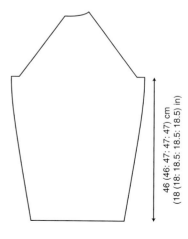

46 (46: 47: 47: 47) cm
(18 (18: 18.5: 18.5: 18.5) in)

30 (30: 32: 32: 34) sts.
Next row (RS): P1, K2tog, K to last 3 sts, K2tog tbl, P1.
Next row: K1, P to last st, K1.
Rep last 2 rows 9 (9: 10: 10: 11) times more. 10 sts.
Left sleeve only
Next row (RS): P1, K2tog, K to last 3 sts, K2tog tbl, P1.
Next row: Cast off 4 sts, P to last st, K1.
Right sleeve only
Next row (RS): Cast off 5 sts (one st on right

needle), K1, K2tog tbl, P1,
Next row: K1, P to end.
Both sleeves
Cast off rem 4 sts.

MAKING UP

PRESS as described on the information page. Join both front and right back raglan seams using back stitch, or mattress st if preferred.
Collar
With RS facing and using 10mm (US 15) needles, pick up and knit 7 sts from left sleeve,

3 sts down left side of neck, 6 (6: 6: 8: 8) sts from front, 3 sts up right side of neck, 7 sts from right sleeve, then 8 (8: 8: 10: 10) sts from back. 34 (34: 34: 38: 38) sts.
Row 1 (WS): P2, *K2, P2, rep from * to end.
Row 2: K2, *P2, K2, rep from * to end.
These 2 rows form rib.
Cont in rib until collar measures 8 cm.
Cast off in rib.
See information page for finishing instructions.
Make a twisted cord approx 130 cm long and thread through eyelet row. Make two 8 cm diameter pompoms and attach to ends of cord.

DESIGN NUMBER 16

MURMUR

KIM HARGREAVES

YARN

	XS-S	S-M	M-L	L-XL	
To fit bust	81-86	86-91	91-97	97-102	cm
	32-34	34-36	36-38	38-40	in

Rowan Biggy Print
8   9   10   11   x 100gm
(photographed in Humbug 254)

NEEDLES
1 pair 20mm (US 36) needles

TENSION
5½ sts and 7 rows to 10 cm measured over stocking stitch using 20mm (US 36) needles.

Pattern note: As row end edges form actual finished front opening edges of garment, it is important these edges are kept neat. Therefore avoid joining in new balls of yarn at these edges.

BACK
Cast on 25 (27: 29: 31) sts using 20mm (US 36) needles.
Beg with a K row, work in st st as folls:
Work 6 rows, ending with a WS row.
Dec 1 st at each end of next and foll 4th Row. 21 (23: 25: 27) sts.
Work 5 rows, ending with a WS row.
Row 17 (RS): K2, M1, K to last 2 sts, M1, K2.
Work 3 rows.
Row 21: As row 17.
25 (27: 29: 31) sts.
Work 5 rows, ending with a WS row. (Back should measure 37 cm.)
Shape armholes
Cast off 2 sts at beg of next 2 rows.
21 (23: 25: 27) sts.
Dec 1 st at each end of next 2 (2: 3: 3) rows.
17 (19: 19: 21) sts.
Cont straight until armhole measures 20 (21: 22: 23) cm, ending with a WS row.
Shape shoulders and back neck
Cast off 2 (3: 2: 3) sts at beg of next 2 rows, then 3 sts at beg of foll row.
Cast off rem 10 (10: 12: 12) sts, placing marker

after 3rd cast-off st to mark other side of back neck.

LEFT FRONT
Cast on 13 (14: 15: 16) sts using 20mm (US 36) needles.
Row 1 (RS): Knit.
Row 2: Purl.
Row 3: K to last st, pick up loop lying between needles and place loop on right needle (**note:** this loop does NOT count as a st), sl next st knitwise.
Row 4: P tog first st and the loop, P to end.
Rows 3 and 4 form st st with slip st edging.
Keeping sts correct as set throughout, cont as folls:
Work 2 rows, ending with a WS row.
Dec 1 st at beg of next and foll 4th Row.
11 (12: 13: 14) sts.
Work 5 rows, ending with a WS row.
Row 17 (RS): K2, M1, patt to end.
12 (13: 14: 15) sts.
Work 3 rows.
Shape front slope
Row 21 (RS): K2, M1, K to last 3 sts, K2tog tbl, patt 1 st. 12 (13: 14: 15) sts.
Working all front slope decreases as set by last row, cont as folls:
Work 5 rows, dec 1 st at front slope edge of 4th of these rows and ending with a WS row.
11 (12: 13: 14) sts.
Shape armhole
Cast off 2 sts at beg of next row. 9 (10: 11: 12) sts.
Work 1 row.

Dec 1 st at armhole edge of next 2 (2: 3: 3) rows **and at same time** dec 0 (0: 1: 1) st at front slope edge of first of these rows.
7 (8: 7: 8) sts.
Dec 1 st at front slope edge **only** of next (next: 2nd: 2nd) and foll 4th row.
5 (6: 5: 6) sts.
Cont straight until left front matches back to start of shoulder shaping, ending with a WS row.
Shape shoulder
Cast off 2 (3: 2: 3) sts at beg of next row.
Work 1 row.
Cast off rem 3 sts.

RIGHT FRONT
Cast on 13 (14: 15: 16) sts using 20mm (US 36) needles.
Row 1 (RS): Knit.
Row 2: P to last st, pick up loop lying between needles and place loop on right needle (**note:** this loop does NOT count as a st), sl next st purlwise.
Row 3: K tog tbl first st and the loop, K to end.
Rows 2 and 3 form st st with slip st edging.
Keeping sts correct as set, cont as folls:
Work 3 rows, ending with a WS row.
Dec 1 st at end of next and foll 4th Row.
11 (12: 13: 14) sts.
Work 5 rows, ending with a WS row.
Row 17 (RS): K2, M1, patt to end.
12 (13: 14: 15) sts.
Work 3 rows.
Shape front slope
Row 21 (RS): Patt 1 st, K2tog, K to last 2 sts, M1, K2. 12 (13: 14: 15) sts.
Working all front slope decreases as set by last row, complete to match left front, reversing shapings.

SLEEVES (both alike)
Cast on 19 (19: 21: 21) sts using 20mm (US 36) needles.
Beg with a K row, cont in st st until sleeve measures 46 (46: 47: 47) cm, ending with a WS row.
Shape top
Cast off 2 sts at beg of next 2 rows.
15 (15: 17: 17) sts.
Dec 1 st at each end of next and every foll alt row until 7 sts rem, then on foll row, ending with a WS row.
Cast off rem 5 sts.

MAKING UP
PRESS as described on the information page. See information page for finishing instructions, setting in sleeves using the set-in method. Attach 45 cm lengths of yarn to front opening edges level with start of front slope shaping to form ties.

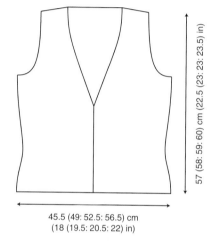

57 (58: 59: 60) cm (22.5 (23: 23: 23.5) in)

45.5 (49: 52.5: 56.5) cm
(18 (19.5: 20.5: 22) in)

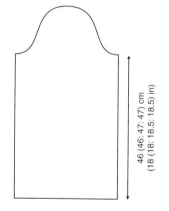

46 (46: 47: 47) cm
(18 (18: 18.5: 18.5) in)

FRAN

KIM HARGREAVES

YARN
One size to fit average size adult
Rowan Biggy Print
2   x   100gm
(photographed in Swirl 250)

NEEDLES
1 pair 15mm (US 19) needles
1 pair 20mm (US 36) needles

TENSION
5 1/2 sts and 7 rows to 10 cm measured over stocking stitch using 20mm (US 36) needles.

COLLAR
Cast on 34 sts using 15mm (US 19) needles.
Row 1 (RS): K2, ★P2, K2, rep from ★ to end.
Row 2: P2, ★K2, P2, rep from ★ to end.
These 2 rows form rib.
Cont in rib until collar measures 12 cm.
Change to 20mm (US 36) needles.
Cont in rib until collar measures 28 cm.
Cast off in rib.

MAKING UP
PRESS as described on the information page.
Join back seam, reversing seam for turn-back.

LILLY

KIM HARGREAVES

YARN
One size to fit average size adult head
Rowan Chunky Print
      1   x   100gm
(photographed in Tart 074 and Girly Pink 077)

HOOK
9.00mm (no 00) crochet hook

TENSION
2 pattern repeats and 5 rows to 10 cm measured over pattern using 9.00mm hook.

CROCHET ABBREVIATIONS
Ch = chain; **ss** = slip stitch; **dc** = double crochet;
tr = treble; **sp** = space.

HAT
Using 9.00mm hook, make 3 ch and join with a ss to form a ring.
Round 1: 1 ch (does NOT count as st), 9 dc into ring, ss to first dc. 9 sts.
Round 2: 1 ch (does NOT count as st), 1 dc into first dc, 1 ch, (1 dc into next dc, 1 ch) 8 times, ss to first dc. 18 sts.
Round 3: 4 ch (counts as first tr and 1 ch), miss first dc, 1 tr into next ch sp, *(1 tr, 1 ch and 1 tr)

into each ch sp to end, ss to 3rd of 4 ch at beg of round. 27 sts.
Round 4: Ss across and into first ch sp, 4 ch (counts as first tr and 1 ch), 1 tr into same ch sp, *1 ch, (1 tr, 1 ch and 1 tr) into next ch sp, rep from * to end, 1 ch, ss to 3rd of 4 ch at beg of round. 36 sts.
Round 5: Ss across and into first ch sp, 4 ch (counts as first tr and 1 ch), 1 tr into same ch sp, *2 ch, (1 tr, 1 ch and 1 tr) into next ch sp, rep from * to end, 2 ch, ss to 3rd of 4 ch at beg of round. 45 sts.
Round 6: Ss across and into first ch sp, 3 ch (counts as first tr), (1 tr, 1 ch and 2 tr) into same

ch sp, *miss next ch sp, (2 tr, 1 ch and 2 tr) into next ch sp, rep from * to end, ss to top of 3 ch at beg of round.
9 patt repeats.
Round 7: Ss across and into first ch sp, 3 ch (counts as first tr), (1 tr, 1 ch and 2 tr) into same ch sp, *miss 4 tr, (2 tr, 1 ch and 2 tr) into next ch sp, rep from * to end, ss to top of 3 ch at beg of round.
Rounds 8 to 11: As round 7.
Fasten off.

MAKING UP
PRESS as described on the information page.

IRIS

KIM HARGREAVES

YARN
Rowan Chunky Print

A Temper	073	2	x	100gm
B Pebble Dash	078	2	x	100gm

HOOK
1 9.00mm (no 00) crochet hook

TENSION
8 sts to 10 cm and 3 rows to 9 cm measured over pattern using 9.00mm hook.

FINISHED SIZE
Completed scarf is approx 21 cm (8½ ins) wide and 228 cm (90 ins) long.

CROCHET ABBREVIATIONS
Ch = chain; **dc** = double crochet;
dtr = double treble.

SCARF
Using 9.00mm hook, make 183 ch **very loosely** using yarn A.
Row 1: 1 dc into 2nd ch from hook, 1 dc into each ch to end, turn. 182 sts.
Row 2: 4 ch (counts as first dtr), 1 dtr into next and every st to end, turn.
This row forms patt.
Join in yarn B.
Using yarn B, patt one row.
Using yarn A, patt one row.
Rep last 2 rows once more.
Break off yarn A and cont using yarn B only.
Patt one row.
Row 8: 1 ch (does NOT count as st), 1 dc into each st to end.
Fasten off.

MAKING UP
PRESS as described on the information page.
Cut 24 lengths of each yarn, each 45 cm long, and knot pairs of these lengths through ends of scarf, placing two knots at the end of each stripe and matching colours.

SWING

KIM HARGREAVES

YARN

One size to fit average size adult head
Rowan Big Wool
2 x 100gm
(photographed in Ice Blue 021)

NEEDLES

1 pair 10mm (no 000) (US 15) needles

TENSION

8½ sts and 13 rows to 10 cm measured over stocking stitch using 10mm (US 15) needles.

HAT

First tie
★★Cast on 3 sts using 10mm (US 15) needles.
Row 1 (RS): Inc in each of first 2 sts, K1. 5 sts.
Row 2: Knit.
Row 3: Inc in first st, K to last 2 sts, inc in next st, K1. 7 sts.
Row 4: K2, P to last 2 sts, K2.
Rows 5 to 8: As rows 3 and 4, twice. 11 sts.
Row 9: Knit.
Row 10: K2, P7, K2.
Rep rows 9 and 10 until tie measures 61 cm, ending with a WS row.★★
Break yarn and leave sts on a holder.

Second tie
Work as given for first tie from ★★ to ★★.
Main section
Next row (RS): Cast on and K 3 sts, knit across 11 sts of second tie, turn and cast on 13 sts, turn and knit across 11 sts of first tie, turn and cast on 3 sts. 41 sts.
Next row: K5, P7, K17, P7, K5.
Next row: Knit.
Rep last 2 rows once more, then first of these 2 rows again, ending with a WS row.
Beg with a K row, work in st st for 16 rows, ending with a WS row.
Shape top
Row 1 (RS): (K7, K3tog) 4 times, K1. 33 sts.
Work 1 row.
Row 3: (K5, K3tog) 4 times, K1. 25 sts.
Work 1 row.
Row 5: (K3, K3tog) 4 times, K1. 17 sts.
Row 6: P1, (P2tog) 4 times.
Break yarn and thread through rem 9 sts. Pull up tight and fasten off securely.

MAKING UP

PRESS as described on the information page. Join back seam using back stitch, or mattress st if preferred. Make 2 twisted cords, each 10 cm long, and two 7 cm diameter pompoms. Attach a pompom to one end of each cord and other end of each cord to ends of ties.

CURLY

KIM HARGREAVES

YARN

Rowan Big Wool
4 x 100gm
(photographed in Swish 022)

NEEDLES

1 pair 15mm (US 19) needles
Cable needle

TENSION

7½ sts and 10 rows to 10 cm measured over stocking stitch using 15mm (US 19) needles.

FINISHED SIZE

Completed scarf is approx 20 cm (8 ins) wide and 250 cm (99 ins) long.

SPECIAL ABBREVIATIONS

C10B = Cable 10 back Slip next 5 sts onto cable needle and leave at back of work, K5, then K5 from cable needle

SCARF

Cast on 15 sts using 15mm (US 19) needles.
Next row (RS): K5, inc once in each of next 5 sts, K5. 20 sts.
Cont in patt as folls:
Row 1 (WS): K5, P10, K5.
Row 2: Knit.
Rep rows 1 and 2, 3 times.
Row 9: As row 1.
Row 10: K5, C10B, K5.
These 10 rows form patt.
Cont in patt until scarf measures approx 250 cm, ending after patt row 9 and with a WS row.
Cast off in pattern, decreasing 5 sts across top of cable.

MAKING UP

PRESS as described on the information page. Darn in ends neatly

GRIT

KIM HARGREAVES

YARN

	XS-S	S-M	M-L	L-XL
To fit bust	81-86	86-91	91-97	97-102	cm
	32-34	34-36	36-38	38-40	in

Rowan Biggy Print

| | 8 | 9 | 10 | 11 | x 100gm |

(photographed in Sheep 258)

NEEDLES

1 pair 20mm (US 36) needles

TENSION

5½ sts and 7 rows to 10 cm measured over stocking stitch using 20mm (US 36) needles.

Pattern note: As row end edges form actual finished armhole and front opening edges of garment, it is important these edges are kept neat. Avoid joining in new balls of yarn at these edges.

BACK

Cast on 28 (30: 32: 34) sts using 20mm (US 36) needles.

Beg with a K row, work in st st as folls:

Work 12 rows, ending with a WS row.

Dec 1 st at each end of next and foll 6th row.

24 (26: 28: 30) sts.

Work 5 rows, ending with a WS row.

Inc 1 st at each end of next and foll 6th row.

28 (30: 32: 34) sts.

Work 3 rows, ending with a WS row. (Back should measure 48 cm.)

Shape armholes

Cast off 2 sts at beg of next 2 rows.

24 (26: 28: 30) sts.

Next row (RS): K1, K2tog, K to last 3 sts, K2tog tbl, pick up loop lying between needles and place loop on right needle (**note**: this loop does NOT count as a st), sl next st knitwise.

Next row: P tog first st and the loop, P2tog tbl, P to last 3 sts, P2tog, pick up loop lying between needles and place loop on right needle (**note**: this loop does NOT count as a st), sl next st purlwise.

Next row (RS): K tog tbl first st and the loop, (K2tog) 0 (1: 1: 1) times, K to last 1 (3: 3: 3) sts, (K2tog tbl) 0 (1: 1: 1) times, pick up loop lying between needles and place loop on right needle, sl next st knitwise.

Last 3 rows form slip st edging and set armhole decreases.

Keeping sts correct as set, dec 1 st at each end of next 0 (0: 0: 1) row. 20 (20: 22: 22) sts.

Cont straight until armhole measures 22 (23: 24: 25) cm, ending with a WS row.

Shape shoulders and back neck

Cast off 3 sts at beg of next 2 rows, then 3 sts at beg of foll row.

Cast off rem 11 (11: 13: 13) sts, placing marker after 3rd cast-off st to mark other side of back neck.

LEFT FRONT

Cast on 14 (15: 16: 17) sts using 20mm (US 36) needles.

Row 1 (RS): Knit.

Row 2: Purl.

Row 3: K to last st, pick up loop lying between needles and place loop on right needle (**note**: this loop does NOT count as a st), sl next st knitwise.

Row 4: P tog first st and the loop, P to end.

Rows 3 and 4 form st st with slip st edging.

Keeping sts correct as set, cont as folls:

Work a further 8 rows, ending with a WS row.

Dec 1 st at beg of next and foll 6th row.

12 (13: 14: 15) sts.

Work 5 rows, ending with a WS row.

Inc 1 st at beg of next and foll 6th row.

14 (15: 16: 17) sts.

Work 1 row, ending with a WS row.

Shape front slope

Next row (RS): K to last 3 sts, K2tog tbl, patt 1 st. 13 (14: 15: 16) sts.

Working all front slope decreases as set by last row, cont as folls:

Work 1 row.

Shape armhole

Cast off 2 sts at beg and dec 0 (0: 1: 0) st at end of next row. 11 (12: 12: 14) sts.

Work 1 row.

Now working slip st edging at **both** ends of rows and all decreases 1 st in from ends of rows, cont as folls:

Dec 1 st at armhole edge of next 2 (3: 3: 4) rows **and at same time** dec 1 st at front slope edge of 1st (1st: 3rd: 1st) of these rows. 8 (8: 8: 9) sts.

Dec 1 st at front slope edge **only** on 3rd (2nd: 4th: next) and every foll 4th row until 6 sts rem.

Cont straight until left front matches back to start of shoulder shaping, ending with a WS row.

Shape shoulder

Cast off 3 sts at beg of next row.

Work 1 row.

Cast off rem 3 sts.

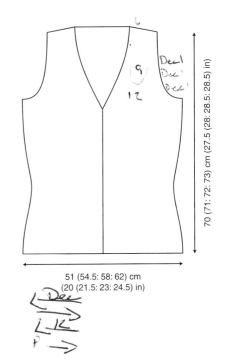

70 (71: 72: 73) cm (27.5 (28: 28.5: 28.5) in)

51 (54.5: 58: 62) cm (20 (21.5: 23: 24.5) in)

RIGHT FRONT

Cast on 14 (15: 16: 17) sts using 20mm (US 36) needles.

Row 1 (RS): Knit.

Row 2: P to last st, pick up loop lying between needles and place loop on right needle (**note:** this loop does NOT count as a st), sl next st purlwise.

Row 3: K tog tbl first st and the loop, K to end.

Rows 2 and 3 form st st with slip st edging.

Keeping sts correct as set, cont as folls:

Work a further 9 rows, ending with a WS row.

Dec 1 st at end of next and foll 6th row.

12 (13: 14: 15) sts.

Work 5 rows, ending with a WS row.

Inc 1 st at end of next and foll 6th row.

14 (15: 16: 17) sts.

Work 1 row, ending with a WS row.

Shape front slope

Next row (RS): Patt 1 st, K2tog, K to end.

13 (14: 15: 16) sts.

Working all front slope decreases as set by last row, complete to match left front, reversing shapings.

MAKING UP

PRESS as described on the information page.

See information page for finishing instructions. Cut 20 cm lengths of yarn and knot pairs of these lengths of yarn through knitting along front slope and back neck edges to form "fur" effect. Across back neck, place knots on every stitch of last row before cast-off. Along front slopes, place knots on every other row and work 2 rows of knots - one row on st next to slip st edging and other row on next st in from edge. Unravel ends of knots to create a more shaggy fringe.

DESIGN NUMBER 23

VIOLET

KIM HARGREAVES

YARN

Rowan Big Wool

4   x   100gm

(photographed in Ice Blue 021)

NEEDLES

1 pair 10mm (no 000) (US 15) needles

TENSION

12 sts and 12 rows to 10 cm measured over pattern using 10mm (US 15) needles.

FINISHED SIZE

Completed bag is approx 35 cm (14 ins) wide and 41 cm (16 ins) deep.

BACK and FRONT (both alike)

Cast on 42 sts using 10mm (US 15) needles.

Row 1 (RS): Purl.

Row 2: P1, ★(K1, P1, K1) all into next st, P3tog, rep from ★ to last st, P1.

Row 3: Purl.

Row 4: P1, ★P3tog, (K1, P1, K1) all into next st, rep from ★ to last st, P1.

These 4 rows form patt.

Cont in patt until work measures 41 cm, ending with a WS row. Cast off.

STRAP

Cast on 7 sts using 10mm (US 15) needles.

Row 1 (RS): Sl 1, (yarn to front, sl 1 purlwise, yarn to back, K1) 3 times.

Row 2: Sl 1, P1, (yarn to back, sl 1 purlwise, yarn to front, P1) twice, K1.

These 2 rows form patt.

Cont in patt until strap measures 90 cm, ending with a WS row.

Cast off.

MAKING UP

PRESS as described on the information page.

Join back and front along row end and **cast-off** edges. Attach ends of strap inside upper edge, over seams.

Flower trim

Using Chunky Print, Deep End 076, make and attach Bloom, see design 14.

DESIGN NUMBER 24

FOSTER

KIM HARGREAVES

YARN

Rowan Big Wool

4   x   100gm

(photographed in Latte 018)

NEEDLES

1 pair 15mm (US 19) needles

TENSION

7½ sts and 10 rows to 10 cm measured over moss stitch using 15mm (US 19) needles.

FINISHED SIZE

Completed scarf is 23 cm (9 ins) wide and 246 cm (97 ins) long.

SCARF

Cast on 17 sts using 15mm (US 19) needles.
Row 1 (RS): K1, (P1, K1) 8 times.
Row 2: As row 1.
These 2 rows form moss st.
Cont in patt until scarf measures 280 cm, ending with a WS row. Cast off in moss st.

MAKING UP

PRESS as described on the information page. Fold 17 cm to RS at each end of scarf and stitch in place along row end edges to form pockets.

COAST

KIM HARGREAVES

YARN

One size to fit average size adult head
Rowan Big Wool
              2   x   100gm
(photographed in Latte 018)

NEEDLES

1 pair 10mm (no 000) (US 15) needles

TENSION

9 sts and 14 rows to 10 cm measured over pattern using 10mm (US 15) needles.

SPECIAL ABBREVIATIONS

Sl 1P = slip one stitch purlwise
M1P = make one stitch by picking up horizontal loop before next stitch and purling into back of it

HAT

Cast on 49 sts using 10mm (US 15) needles.
Row 1 (RS): P1, (sl 1P, P3) 12 times.
Row 2: (K3, P1) 12 times, K1.
Rows 3 and 4: As rows 1 and 2.
Row 5: P1, ★sl 1P, (P1, M1P) twice, P1, sl 1P, P3, rep from ★ to end. 61 sts.
Row 6: ★K3, P1, K5, P1; rep from ★ to last st, K1.
Row 7: P1, (sl 1P, P5, sl 1P, P3) 6 times.
Row 8: As row 6.
Row 9: P1, (sl 1P, P5, sl 1P, P2, M1P, P1) 6 times. 67 sts.
Row 10: ★K4, P1, K5, P1, rep from ★ to last st, K1.
Row 11: P1, (sl 1P, P5, sl 1P, P4) 6 times.
Rows 12 to 19: As rows 10 and 11, 4 times.
Row 20: As row 10.
Row 21: P1, (sl 1P, P3, P2tog, sl 1P, P4) 6 times. 61 sts.
Row 22: ★K4, P1, rep from ★ to last st, K1.
Row 23: P1, (sl 1P, P4) 12 times.
Row 24: As row 22.
Row 25: P1, (sl 1P, P2, P2tog) 12 times. 49 sts.
Row 26: As row 2.
Rows 27 and 28: As rows 1 and 2.
Row 29: P1, (sl 1P, P1, P2tog) 12 times. 37 sts.
Row 30: ★K2, P1, rep from ★ to last st, K1.
Row 31: P1, (sl 1P, P2tog) 12 times. 25 sts.
Row 32: ★K1, P1, rep from ★ to last st, K1.
Row 33: P1, (sl 1 **knitwise**, K1, psso) 12 times.
Break yarn and thread through rem 13 sts. Pull up tight and fasten off securely.

MAKING UP

PRESS as described on the information page. Join back seam using back stitch, or mattress st if preferred.
Darn in ends neatly

POPPY

KIM HARGREAVES

YARN

Rowan Chunky Print
              4   x   100gm
(photographed in Swizzle 075)

HOOK

6.00mm (no 4) (US J10) crochet hook
9.00mm (no 00) crochet hook

TENSION

2 pattern repeats and 5 rows to 10 cm measured over pattern using 9.00mm hook.

FINISHED SIZE

Completed bag is approx 35 cm (14 ins) wide and 41 cm (16 ins) deep.

CROCHET ABBREVIATIONS

Ch = chain; **ss** = slip stitch; **dc** = double crochet; **tr** = treble.

MAIN SECTION

Using 9.00mm hook, make 67 ch and join with a ss to form a ring, ensuring ch is not twisted.
Round 1: 1 ch (does NOT count as st), 1 dc into first ch, ★miss 2 ch, 5 tr into next ch, miss 2 ch, 1 dc into next ch, rep from ★ to end.

Round 2: 3 ch (counts as first tr), 2 tr into st at base of 3 ch, ★miss 2 tr, 1 dc into next tr, miss 2 tr, 5 tr into next dc, rep from ★ to end, ending last rep with 2 tr into last dc, ss to top of 3 ch at beg of round.
Round 3: 1 ch (does NOT count as st), 1 dc into first tr, ★miss 2 tr, 5 tr into next dc, miss 2 tr, 1 dc into next tr, rep from ★ to end, ss to first dc.
Rep rounds 2 and 3 until work measures 52 cm. Fasten off.

STRAP
Using 6.00mm hook, make 6 ch.
Row 1: 1 dc into 2nd ch from hook, 1 dc into

each of next 4 ch, turn. 5 sts.
Row 2: 1 ch (does NOT count as st), 1 dc into each dc to end, turn.
Rep row 2 until strap measures 105 cm. Fasten off.

MAKING UP
PRESS as described on the information page. Lay main section flat and sew base (foundation ch) seam.
Place ends of strap onto back of main section, positioning edges of straps next to folds and ends of straps 22 cm up from base seam, and sew straps to main section for first 6 cm of strap. (Opening of bag will flop over to front to form flap.)

DESIGN NUMBER 27

S P I K E

KIM HARGREAVES

YARN
	S	M	L		
Rowan Big Wool					
	1	1	1	x	100gm

(photographed in Smudge 019 and Best Brown 027)

NEEDLES
1 pair 10mm (no 000) (US 15) needles

TENSION
8½ sts and 13 rows to 10 cm measured over rib pattern using 10mm (US 15) needles.

HAT
Cast on 37 (41: 45) sts using 10mm (US 15) needles.
Row 1 (RS): ★K2, P2, rep from ★ to last st, K1.
Row 2: P1, ★K2, P2, rep from ★ to end.
These 2 rows form rib.
Work in rib for a further 16 rows, ending with a WS row.
Beg with a P row, cont in rev st st as folls:
Work 2 rows, ending with a WS row.
Shape top
Small and large sizes only
Row 1 (RS): (P7 (-: 9), P2tog) 4 times, P1. 33 (-: 41) sts.
Work 1 row.
Medium and large sizes only
Next row (RS): (P7, P3tog) 4 times, P1. 33 sts.
Work 1 row.
All sizes
Next row (RS): (P5, P3tog) 4 times, P1. 25 sts.
Next row: K1, (K3tog, K3) 4 times.
Break yarn and thread through rem 17 sts. Pull up tight and fasten off securely.

MAKING UP
PRESS as described on the information page.
Darn in ends neatly
Join back seam using back stitch, or mattress st if preferred.

DESIGN NUMBER 28

G A B Y

KIM HARGREAVES

YARN
One size to fit average size adult head
Rowan Big Wool
A	Blue Velvet	026	1	x	100gm
B	Wild Berry	025	1	x	100gm

NEEDLES
1 pair 10mm (no 000) (US 15) needles

TENSION
7 sts and 18 rows to 10 cm measured over rib pattern using 10mm (US 15) needles.

SPECIAL ABBREVIATION
K1 below = Knit into st directly below next st on left needle, slipping st above off left needle at same time

HAT
Cast on 33 sts using 10mm (US 15) needles and yarn A.
Knit 1 row.
Cont in rib patt as folls:
Row 1 (RS): Sl 1, ★K1 below, K1, rep from ★ to end.
Row 2: Sl 1, K1, ★K1 below, K1, rep from ★ to last st, K1.

These 2 rows form rib patt.
Cont in rib patt until work measures 12 cm, ending with a WS row.
Break off yarn A and join in yarn B.
Cont in rib patt until work measures 23 cm, ending with a **RS** row.

Shape top
Row 1 (WS): (Patt 3 sts, K3tog) 5 times, patt 3 sts. 23 sts.
Work 5 rows.
Row 7: Patt 3 sts, (K3tog, patt 1 st) 5 times. 13 sts.
Purl 1 row.
Break yarn and thread through rem 13 sts. Pull up tight and fasten off securely.

MAKING UP

PRESS as described on the information page.
Join back seam using back stitch, or mattress st if preferred, reversing seam for turn-back.

CRUMBLE

KIM HARGREAVES

YARN
One size to fit average size adult
Rowan Chunky Print
            1   x   100gm
(photographed in Tart 074)

NEEDLES
1 pair 8mm (no 0) (US 11) needles

TENSION
11 sts and 14 rows to 10 cm measured over flattened rib pattern using 8mm (US 11) needles.

Pattern note:
To ensure there is sufficient yarn for both wrist warmers the yarn needs to be equally divided in two. To do this, work the first wrist warmer taking the yarn from the **outside** of the ball. Stop at the point specified and then work the second wrist warmer taking the yarn from the **inside** of the ball.

LEFT WRIST WARMER
Taking yarn from **outside** of ball, cast on 30 sts using 8mm (US 11) needles.
Row 1 (RS): K2, ★P2, K2, rep from ★ to end.
Row 2: P2, ★K2, P2, rep from ★ to end.
These 2 rows form rib.
Work in rib for a further 2 rows.
Make thumb hole
Row 5 (RS): Rib 18, cast off 2 sts, rib to end.
Row 6: Rib to end, casting on 2 sts over those cast off on previous row.
Cont in rib until work measures approx 26 cm.
Leave these sts on a spare needle. Do **NOT** break yarn.

RIGHT WRIST WARMER
Taking yarn from **inside** of ball, cast on 30 sts using 8mm (US 11) needles.
Work in rib as given for left wrist warmer for 4 rows.
Make thumb hole
Row 5 (RS): Rib 10, cast off 2 sts, rib to end.
Row 6: Rib to end, casting on 2 sts over those cast off on previous row.
Cont in rib until work measures same as left wrist warmer.
Divide rem yarn into two and cut yarn so that each wrist warmer has same amount of rem yarn.
Cont in rib until all yarn has been used up, leaving sufficient to cast-off. Cast off in rib.
Now complete left wrist warmer to match.

MAKING UP
PRESS as described on the information page.
Join seam.

FROTHY

KIM HARGREAVES

YARN
Rowan Chunky Print
            6   x   100gm
(photographed in Tart 074)

HOOK
9.00mm (no 00) crochet hook
TENSION
2 pattern repeats to 14 cm and 4 rows to 12 cm measured over pattern using 9.00mm hook.

FINISHED SIZE
Completed scarf is 28 cm (11 ins) wide and 300 cm (118 ins) long.

CROCHET ABBREVIATIONS
Ch = chain; **tr** = treble; **sp** = space.

SCARF
Using 9.00mm hook, make 32 ch.
Row 1: 1 tr into 5th ch from hook, (2 ch, miss 5 ch, 4 tr into next ch, 2 ch, 1 tr into next ch) 3 times, 2 ch, miss 5 ch, 4 tr into last ch, turn.
Row 2: 4 ch, 1 tr into tr at end of last row, 2 ch, miss (3 tr, 2 ch and 1 tr), ★(4 tr, 2 ch and 1 tr) into next ch sp, 2 ch, miss (4 tr, 2 ch and 1 tr), rep from ★ twice more, 4 tr into top of 4 ch at

beg of previous row, turn.
Rep row 2 until scarf measures 300 cm.
Fasten off.

MAKING UP

PRESS as described on the information page.
Cut 90 lengths of each yarn, each 40 cm long, and knot groups of 5 of these lengths through ends of scarf, placing 9 knots evenly across each end.

DESIGN NUMBER 31

HUDDLE

KIM HARGREAVES

YARN

Rowan Biggy Print and Chunky Print

1st colourway

A	BiggyP	Allsorts 255	3	x	100gm
B	ChunkyP	Tart 074	1	x	100gm

2nd colourway

A	BiggyP	Savage 256	3	x	100gm
B	ChunkyP	Temper 073	1	x	100gm

NEEDLES

1 pair 20mm (US 36) needles

TENSION

5½ sts and 7 rows to 10 cm measured over stocking stitch using 20mm (US 36) needles.

FINISHED SIZE

Completed scarf is approx 15 cm (6 ins) wide and 190 cm (75 ins) long.

SCARF

Cast on 12 sts using 20mm (US 36) needles and yarn A.
Row 1 (WS): Using yarn A, knit.
Row 2: Using yarn A, inc purlwise in first st, P to last 2 sts, P2tog.
Join in yarn B.
Row 3: Using yarn B, knit.
Row 4: Using yarn B, inc purlwise in first st, P to last 2 sts, P2tog.
These 4 rows form patt.
Cont in patt until scarf measures approx 190 cm, ending after patt row 2 and with a WS row.
Cast off.

MAKING UP

PRESS as described on the information page.

Photographer Joey Toller
Styling Kim Hargreaves
Hair & Make-up Annabel Hobbs
Models Lauren, Alicia and Niran
Reproduction in whole or any part of all material, including illustrations, in this publication is strictly forbidden unless prior consent of the publisher has been given in writing. Yarn quantities are approximate as they are based on average requirements. Colour reproduction is as close as printing will allow.
Copyright Rowan 2003

INFORMATION PAGE

TENSION

Obtaining the correct tension is perhaps the single factor which can make the difference between a successful garment and a disastrous one. It controls both the shape and size of an article, so **any** variation, can distort the finished look of the garment. We recommend that you knit a square in pattern and/or stocking stitch of perhaps 5 more stitches and rows than those given in the tension note. Press the finished square under a damp cloth and mark out the central 10cm square. If you have too many stitches to 10cm try again using thicker needles, if you have too few stitches to 10cm try again using finer needles.

SIZING AND SIZE DIAGRAM NOTE

The instructions are given for the smallest size. Where they vary, work the figures in brackets for the larger sizes. **One set of figures refers to all sizes.** Included with every pattern in this magazine is a '**size diagram**', the purpose of which is to enable you to accurately achieve a perfect fitting garment without the need for worry during knitting. The size diagram shows the finished width of the garment at the under-arm point, and it is this measurement that the knitter should choose first. Next look at the corresponding length for that size; if you are not happy with the total length which we recommend, adjust your own garment before beginning your armhole shaping - any adjustment after this point will mean that your sleeve will not fit into your garment easily - don't forget to take your adjustment into account if there is any side seam shaping. Finally, look at the sleeve length; the size diagram shows the finished sleeve measurement, taking into account any top-arm insertion length. Measure your body between the centre of your neck and your wrist, this measurement should correspond to half the garment width plus the sleeve length. Again, your sleeve length may be adjusted, but remember to take into consideration your sleeve increases if you do adjust the length - you must increase more frequently than the pattern states to shorten your sleeve, less frequently to lengthen it.

FINISHING INSTRUCTIONS

After working for hours knitting a garment, it seems a great pity that many garments are spoiled because such little care is taken in the pressing and finishing process.

PRESSING

Darn in all ends neatly along the selvage edge or a colour join, as appropriate. Block out each piece of knitting using pins and gently press each piece, omitting the ribs, using a warm iron over a damp cloth. **Tip**: Take special care to press the edges, as this will make sewing up both easier and neater.

STITCHING

When stitching the pieces together, remember to match areas of colour and texture very carefully where they meet.
Use a seam stitch such as back stitch or mattress stitch for all main knitting seams, and join all ribs and neckband with a flat seam unless otherwise stated.

CONSTRUCTION

Having completed the pattern instructions, join left shoulder and neckband seams as detailed above. Sew the top of the sleeve to the body of the garment using the method detailed in the pattern, referring to the appropriate guide:

Square set-in sleeves: Set sleeve head into armhole, the straight sides at top of sleeve to form a neat right-angle to cast-off sts at armhole on back and front.

Shallow set-in sleeves: Join cast-off sts at beg of armhole shaping to cast-off sts at start of sleeve-head shaping. Sew sleeve head into armhole, easing in shapings.

Set-in sleeves: Set in sleeve, easing sleeve head into armhole.

JOIN SIDE AND SLEEVE SEAMS.

Slip stitch pocket edgings and linings into place. Sew on buttons to correspond with buttonholes. After sewing up, press seams and hems. Ribbed welts and neckbands and any areas of garter stitch should not be pressed.

ABBREVIATIONS

K	knit
P	purl
st(s)	stitch(es)
inc	increas(e)(ing)
dec	decreas(e)(ing)
st st	stocking stitch (1 row K, 1 row P)
garter st	garter stitch (K every row)
beg	begin(ning)
foll	following
rem	remain(ing)
rev	revers(e)(ing)
rep	repeat
alt	alternate
cont	continue
patt	pattern
tog	together
mm	millimetres
cm	centimetres
in(s)	inch(es)
RS	right side
WS	wrong side
sl1	slip one stitch
psso	pass slipped stitch over
p2sso	pass 2 slipped stitches over
tbl	through back of loop
M1	make one stitch by picking up horizontal loop before next stitch and knitting into back of it
yfwd	yarn forward
yrn	yarn round needle
yon	yarn over needle
cn	cable needle

EXPERIENCE RATINGS

 = Easy, straight forward knitting

 = Suitable for the average knitter

STOCKIST INFORMATION

ROWAN OVERSEAS DISTRIBUTORS

AUSTRALIA
Australian Country Spinners
314 Albert Street,
Brunswick
Victoria 3056.
Tel: (03) 9380 3888

BELGIUM
Pavan
Koningin Astridlaan 78,
B9000 Gent
Tel: (32) 9 221 8594

CANADA
Diamond Yarn
9697 St Laurent,
Montreal
Quebec H3L 2N1
Tel: (514) 388 6188
www.diamondyarns.com

Diamond Yarn (Toronto)
155 Martin Ross,
Unit 3
Toronto,
Ontario M3J 2L9
Tel: (416) 736 6111
www.diamondyarns.com

DENMARK
Individual stockists –
please contact Rowan for details

FRANCE
Elle Tricot
8 Rue du Coq
67000 Strasbourg
Tel: (33) 3 88 23 03 13
www.elletricote.com

GERMANY
Wolle & Design
Wolfshovener Strasse 76
52428 Julich-Stetternich
Tel : (49) 2461 54735.
www.wolleundesign.de

HOLLAND
de Afstap
Oude Leliestraat 12
1015 AW Amsterdam
Tel : (31) 20 6231445

HONG KONG
East Unity Co Ltd
Unit B2
7/F, Block B
Kailey Industrial Centre
12 Fung Yip Street
Chai Wan
Tel : (852) 2869 7110.

ICELAND
Storkurinn
Kjorgardi
Laugavegi 59
Reykjavik
Tel: (354) 551 82 58

JAPAN
Puppy Co Ltd
TOC Building
7-22-17 Nishigotanda
Shinagwa-Ku
Tokyo
Tel : (81) 3 3494 2395

NEW ZEALAND
Individual stockists –
please contact Rowan for details

NORWAY
Pa Pinne
Tennisun 3D
0777 OSLO
Tel: (47) 909 62 818
www.paapinne.no

SWEDEN
Wincent
Norrtulsgaten 65
11345 Stockholm
Tel: (46) 8 673 70 60

U.S.A.
Rowan USA
4 Townsend West
Suite 8
Nashua
New Hampshire 03063
Tel: (1 603) 886 5041/5043

For details of U.K. stockists or any other information concerning this book please contact:

Rowan Yarns, Green Lane Mill, Holmfirth, West Yorkshire HD9 2DX
Tel: +44 (0)1484 681881   Fax: +44 (0)1484 687920
Email: nextbigthing@knitrowan.com www.knitrowan.com